Leading with the Social Brain in Mind

Dr Joanne Casey

Leading with the Social Brain in Mind

Cognition, complexity
and collaboration in schools

Praise for *Leading with the Social Brain in Mind*

In these stressful times, it is important to deliberately pause and consider the impact of 'cognitive overload' in our daily optimal functioning. Dr Joanne Casey's new and original thinking, *Leading with the Social Brain in Mind*, is a 'must read' for all educators striving to give all students the best possible life chances, amid the turbulence in society. Joanne gives teachers and leaders many practical strategies to meet the demands of ensuring that ALL students are growing and achieving. Pure gold.

Dr Lyn Sharratt – Honorary Fellow, University of Melbourne, Graduate School of Education, International Consultant and Author

The provocations are powerful! *Leading with the Social Brain in Mind* clearly shows us that we must have a more realistic understanding of the organisational structures we create in our schools. School improvement requires more than a framework or a revised approach.

Leanne Armao – Principal, Keysborough Primary School, Vic

Leading with the Social Brain in Mind connects the lived experience with research. In particular, the visuals helped me to conceptualise my own thinking. I really liked the mapping approach at the end of each chapter – it makes lots of sense to me.

Scott Moore – Head of Junior School Burgmann Anglican School, ACT

Joanne clearly explains the complex nature of collaboration within the schooling context, recognizing the mental gymnastics we go through every day! The questions she places at the end of each chapter brings focus and attention to assumptions at play, encouraging exploration and dialogue.

Debra Patzwald – Experienced Senior Teacher, Darling Downs, QLD

Joanne, thank you for writing the section about Wardley Mapping. And yes… maps are not solutions, nor are they ever right. They are a graphical communication tool – a way of having conversations around complex and complicated spaces.

Simon Wardley – British Researcher and former CEO, best known for the creation of Wardley Mapping

Published in 2023 by Amba Press, Melbourne, Australia
www.ambapress.com.au

© Joanne Casey 2023

All rights reserved. No part of this book may be reproduced or transmitted in any form or by any means, electronic or mechanical, including photocopying, recording or by any information storage and retrieval system, without prior permission in writing from the publisher.

Cover design: Tess McCabe
Internal design: Amba Press
Editor: Rica Dearman
Printing: IngramSpark

ISBN: 9781922607706 (pbk)
ISBN: 9781922607713 (ebk)

A catalogue record for this book is available from the National Library of Australia.

Contents

Acknowledgements		1
About the author		3
Introduction		5
Chapter 1	Leading with the Social Brain in Mind	21
Chapter 2	Schools as complex organisations	41
Chapter 3	Collaboration is socially and cognitively more complex than first thought	61
Chapter 4	Organisational cultures and differentiated relationships	79
Chapter 5	Silo mentality as a construct of function, knowledge and experience	95
Chapter 6	Implications for policy and practice	117
Chapter 7	Mapping situational context with Wardley Mapping	139
Conclusion		151
References		153

Acknowledgements

A colleague once told me that completing a PhD was an exercise in persistence and resilience. That is true. Writing a book based on *that* PhD is an interesting exercise, too. Those who know me well, understand that writing is not my *preferred* form of communication. While writing this book has been less arduous (for the most part) than writing the thesis, there are similar qualities employed to get the job done. Most importantly, both endeavours saw people surrounding/enveloping me with support and encouragement along the way. This type of involvement cannot be underestimated, and so I would like to acknowledge their contributions in making *this* particular dream a reality.

Once again, I would first like to thank my wonderful husband, Ray, who always supports my pursuits in multiple ways. On this occasion, he has actively encouraged me to lose myself in the 'luxury' of uninterrupted opportunities to think and engage in adjusting, translating and transferring key ideas and concepts from one audience to another. I would also like to express my deep gratitude to my family. My parents – Dell and Norm – and sister, Trish, your unwavering support and confidence in me to *get the job done* always brings a smile to my face. Jason, Thomas, Nathan, Caitlin, Jess, Kate and Nick, thank you for engaging in lengthy conversations about education, schools, teaching, learning and all things about the brain! My grandchildren – you are the light of my life and my motivation for why I continue to do what I do.

Next, thank you to those wonderful participants who contributed to my study and were the catalyst for this book. Your voices shine a light on the very real issues associated with expectations for collaborative interactions and how this is undertaken in schools. Although the study was undertaken in secondary school contexts, many other colleagues in primary contexts assure me that what is highlighted here is the same for them.

Dr Selena Fisk – you are an inspiration, and without your introduction to the wonderful Alicia Cohen, this book would still be ruminating and rattling around my brain! The right publisher is a gift. Alicia, thank you for navigating me through the publishing process. I am grateful for your professionalism and dedication, but in particular, I treasure your warmth and patience in steering the way forward for a novice author.

I am indebted to my editor, Rica Dearman, for her insightful comments and expert guidance. Her suggestions and revisions helped me to share my thinking with more clarity and cohesiveness.

To my colleagues, you provided valuable feedback and encouragement throughout the writing process. Conversations in hallways, classrooms and offices energise me in ways that move my thinking forward and keep me searching for possibilities. I would particularly like to thank those who accepted my invitation to read through certain chapters or decided to continue to read the entire manuscript! Your insights and wisdom make this piece of work stronger and applicable to a range of school contexts.

- Leanne Armao – Principal, Keysborough Primary School, Vic
- Trevor Durbidge – Deputy Principal, Bli Bli State School, QLD
- Dr Selena Fisk – Data storyteller, author, speaker, facilitator
- Scott Moore – Head of Junior School Burgmann Anglican School, ACT
- Debra Patzwald – Experienced senior teacher (secondary school), Darling Downs, QLD
- Dr Grace Quaglio – Advisor, mentor, educator, *Informing & Inspiring Special Learning through Music*
- Simon Wardley – British researcher and former CEO, best known for the creation of Wardley Mapping
- Dr Lyn Sharratt – Mentor, colleague and friend.

About the author

Joanne Casey is an education practitioner who works in a range of contexts to support reform agendas that build sustainable practices over time. Her focus remains on improved outcomes for ALL students. She understands schools are complex environments requiring flexible but research-based approaches to achieve improved outcomes for those they serve.

Introduction

Why read this book (purpose)

The work of educators has increased exponentially over past years, and the notion of "heavy hours", as described by Beck (2017, p617), highlights fast-paced, minute-to-minute professional decision-making with being pulled in multiple directions simultaneously during face-to-face (and online) classroom teaching. The assumption here is that if not face to face with students or others, then these 'hours' could be considered 'lighter'. Unfortunately, anyone who works in schools might challenge this assumption. I would also argue that increased expectations to collaborate have created both benefits and unforeseen costs to the individual and the organisation. Please don't misunderstand me – collaboration within and beyond schools is a crucial component that is highly undervalued because of the tensions it creates in the way we currently organise schools.

This brings me to the purpose for writing this book. If you have encountered, or are familiar with, any of the following, then this book might be a way forward for you and your teams:

1. Is whole-school improvement a matter of balancing multiple initiatives and multiple demands with multiple teams?
2. Is collaboration highly valued in your context, but difficult to coordinate and structure within the time frames you have available?
3. Are teams, or an individual's geographical location, making collaboration challenging?

4. Do you have strong vertical or horizontal collaboration within subject departments/sectors, but these often seem loosely coupled to whole-school goals and initiatives?
5. Do different departments see themselves in competition for available financial, technical and human resources?
6. Are your teams short on the time, energy and/or skill that it takes to lead collaborative initiatives?
7. Do your school structures make collaboration problematic?
8. Has your school grown larger over time and do the processes that worked for a smaller school no longer work now?
9. Do you see collaboration working more informally in your context?
10. Are you still building shared understanding or skill sets to lead the types of collaboration that you think will work best in your context?

What this book is and what it is not

- It is a starting point.
- It is an invitation to *foreground the social brain* when thinking about schools and the work we do in them.
- It is an opportunity to *explore possibilities* for why we might *underestimate the social and cognitive complexity* in collaborative interactions in schools.

- It is *not* a recipe.
- It is *not* a one-size-fits-all.
- It is *not* context specific.

Framing up each chapter

In framing up each chapter it was important for me to design them in a way that supported individual and collective thinking about key ideas and processes. This meant reflecting on my own beliefs about learning and why I would set a book out in this manner. While I would hope that you take up these ideas and *contextualise them for your own contexts*, essentially, this book is an invitation to frame your own learning and seek alternative ways to consider problems or issues that can occur when siloing evidence informs our practices. In other words, as leaders in schools, it is critical to carve out time to *identify and reflect on the assumptions* that can underpin the practices we employ in the name of improving student outcomes. In that vein, here are some beliefs that are inherent in the design of the chapter format. These beliefs are based on a culmination and, in some cases, adaptations of educational theories from key educators that have influenced me profoundly in my practices as an educator and as a research practitioner…

1. *Knowledge and experience about topics* varies person to person.
2. *Background knowledge shapes* what we bring to the text and how we might engage (or not) with it.
3. Making the process of accessing and building on background knowledge *transparent* is important for processing what we know, what we don't know and what we will do with what we know. Put another way, how will we recognise if what is being presented is new content?
4. *Deepening* our understanding is important so that we can change, adjust, adapt or add to current knowledge. In some cases, we might need to remove pieces or chunks of what we knew to be true. Revising our understanding of concepts, processes and actions is exceptionally important as we lead change agendas. It provides us with the opportunities to correct misconceptions, identify and address unforeseen or unrecognised issues and gaps.
5. *Articulating reasons* for amending our prior understandings models the importance of a more open-minded and flexible approach to problem-solving, which can be valuable in a world that is constantly changing.
6. Lastly, in applying what we know to new situations, we are able to *make connections, think and design novel and innovative solutions to complex problems*.

Each chapter begins with a graphic (see overleaf) that seeks to bring your attention to key ideas that you may or may not be familiar with. If you are familiar with certain concepts, you are invited to contemplate how you might extend your understanding and apply them in your context. At the same time, you are asked to reflect on decisions (or possible decisions) and how these have or are being impacted by implementation barriers and/or levers for change. Most importantly, now that you and your teams have this knowledge, what might you *do differently* to support those undertaking this work in schools?

New to me
- Draw attention to key ideas
- Make connections to concepts
- Encourage you to reflect on your own context

Revisiting, reviewing and revising familiar ideas
- Encourage you to revisit key ideas and think about how these might be deepened through your own questions or insights
- Suggest you review your current practices or processes
- Provoke you to revise or renew current thinking

Applying in unfamiliar, different or alternative contexts
- Seek ways to adapt, modify or adopt for your context
- Reflect and deliberate on choices
- Consider implementation barriers or levers
- Provoke new ways of thinking

Each chapter then unfolds in the following manner:

1. **Provocation** – quote or question to stimulate connections and thinking.
2. **Key points** – bring attention to ideas that could be unfamiliar but important for the work we undertake in schools.
3. **Links to research, policy and practice** – why these ideas matter for you, your staff and the students you serve.
4. **Leading schools requires additional and different types of knowledge, training and professional experience** – contextualising these ideas has implications for preparing school leaders.
5. **Conclusion** – summary.
6. **Mapping next steps** – processes to put these ideas into practice.

Definitions

> "Watch your thoughts, they become your words; watch your words, they become your actions; watch your actions, they become your habits; watch your habits, they become your character; watch your character, it becomes your destiny."
>
> – ATTRIBUTED TO LAO TZU OR GANDHI

Have you ever been to a social gathering with people from a different industry? It's not too long before you hear certain terms and phrases being tossed around that are familiar, but you get a sense that maybe they are not being used in the same way that educators use them. Maybe you have moved from one school system to another and in those first few months you hear many of the same terms you know from the previous schools you have worked in, but you are *not entirely sure* that they are being used in the same way.

People's knowledge of any topic is encapsulated in the terms and concepts they know are relevant to that topic. Yet my own experience (and study), on more than one occasion, shines a light on words and phrases having multiple meanings and often being used interchangeably. Unfortunately, missteps, misconceptions and misunderstandings have followed genuine attempts to communicate ideas practically and in real time.

I have become achingly aware that words are not neutral, nor is there a common language used for the discourse surrounding education practices. Words shape meaning and meaning is shaped by the words we use (or do not use), when and how we use them. That being said, I acknowledge the same for many of the terms used in this book and which is why I thought it important to foreground and define terms being used here. It is with hope that this provides greater clarification and shared understanding for the ideas being presented.

School Improvement

A continual, sustained and systematic process of making changes in the learning conditions to a school to increase student achievement. It involves identifying areas that need improvement, developing a plan of action and implementing the plan to make positive changes.

School improvement can include, but is not limited to, changes to organisational structures, culture, curriculum, instruction and assessment. It is an ongoing process that can involve teachers, school leaders, parents and other stakeholders in the school community.

Collaboration

This is a process that involves people working together with an emphasis on common goals, relationships and mutual interdependence as a way of improving schools, teacher quality and student achievement (DuFour & Reeves, 2016; Musanti & Pence, 2010; Sharratt & Planche, 2016; Slater, 2004; Vangrieken et al., 2015). Although collaborative practices can be viewed along a continuum – informal to formal – there is a difference between cooperation and collaboration. Sifting through different definitions and comparisons leads me to conceptualise it in this way...

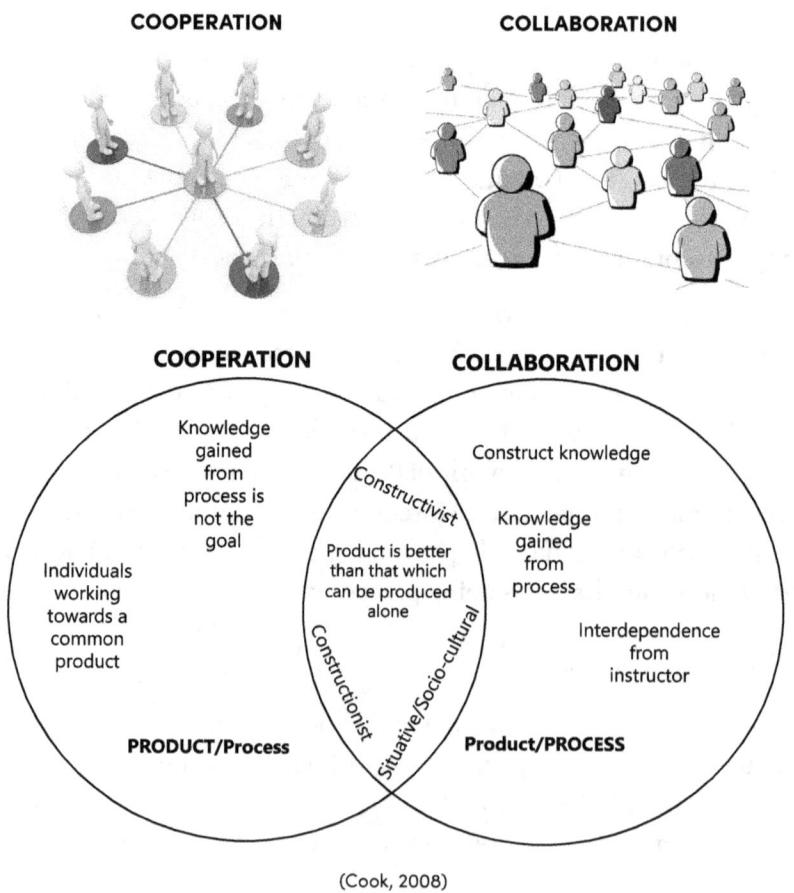

(Cook, 2008)

Silo Mentality

Silos are used as organisational metaphors to describe key aspects of a cultural phenomenon, that collectively result in barriers – psychological and physical – based on our human need to classify and organise social and mental models (Tett, 2016). In her book, *The Silo Effect: Why Every Organisation Needs to Disrupt Itself to Survive*, Gillian Tett suggests that silos are a consequence of how we respond to what can be described as "chaos" when working in complex organisations. Silos provide the structure to cope with this chaos. No business, institution or government agency is immune from silo mentality in which barriers develop among the organisation's many parts (Forsten-Astikainen et al., 2017; Lloyd, 2016; Tett, 2016). The 'parts' are usually well-defined by their function and their focus is geared towards achieving their own objectives rather than how these fit within the larger organisation (Haywood-Matty, 2007; Stone, 2004). Therefore, silo mentality refers to a phenomenon that results in the absence of systemic thinking, or a big picture vision of the larger organisation. Silos can have alluring qualities that make them difficult to recognise as being problematic for the individual, team or organisation.

Social Brain Theory

This refers to a quantitative relationship between social-group size (number) and neocortex volume (Dunbar, 1998). This relationship predicts a group size of approximately 150 for humans at any given time and appears to be the typical size of both social communities in small-scale societies and personal social networks in the modern world (Dunbar, 1998, 2014a, 2014b). Energy, attention and effort are given to those closest, hence networks being described as layered.

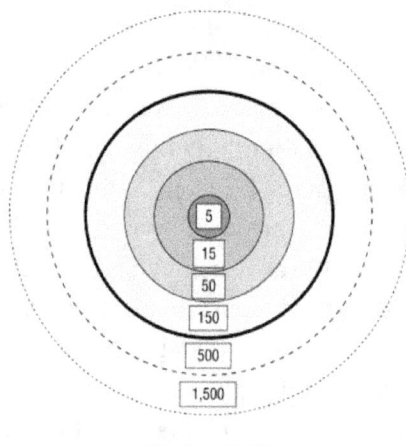

(Dunbar, 2014)

With each increasing layer, emotional connectedness decreases – thus illustrating a correlation between the size of social networks and individuals' mentalising abilities (Dunbar et al., 2015; Mac Carron et al., 2016). In other words, the more social connections a person has, the more cognitive resources they need to maintain those relationships, and there is a point at which the brain experiences cognitive fatigue.

Social Capital Theory

The social structure, or the network of relationships among individuals, offers opportunities and constraints for the exchange of resources (Hargreaves, 2012; Vorhaus, 2014). Social capital, therefore, resides in the nature and quality of the relationships within an organisation rather than in the individuals themselves (Hargreaves, 2012; Jones & Harris, 2014). It is viewed as an asset when actively understood and managed appropriately. Collaboration is often employed to harness social capital.

Theory of Mind

Theory of mind is the ability to understand that other people have different beliefs, thoughts and intentions to oneself. It is the ability to comprehend that others may not think the same way as oneself, and to be able to take another person's perspective into account when making decisions. Theory of mind is an important part of social cognition and is essential for successful communication and collaboration.

Values and beliefs that underpin this work

There are a number of values and beliefs that position the work of this book. My personal and professional perspectives are shaped (or misshaped) by more than 30 years across three education systems (Catholic, Independent and Government), working as a classroom teacher and leader in curriculum, pedagogy and literacy in primary and secondary school contexts. The school contexts were varied – large, small, city, rural and regional. There were periods of time when I worked as a consultant across Australia, a sessional academic and school-based leader – all at the same time. My roles varied from one school context to the next. Sometimes it was as mentor and coach for school leaders and lead teachers, and sometimes it was as a 'guide on the side' for classroom teachers.

At all times my work involved supporting and assisting educators as they planned clear, actionable and achievable steps to support student growth through leveraging teacher practices (including the development and/or implementation of their own pedagogical or instructional frameworks). These were most interesting times. While I was able to engage in learning with and from key experts in the education field and then put research into practice, there was never a time that these were replicated exactly in any school. In other words, evidence-based practices were informing implementation decisions, but they were not being carbon copied. If I didn't have the belief beforehand, I certainly came to live and breathe it – a one-size-fits-all approach does not work. This was made more obvious as I took dual roles of being an *insider-outsider* and vice versa.

The importance of *insider-outsider* experience and knowledge

An *insider-outsider*, in this context, is someone who has worked in schools as an educator and understands how they operate but is not employed by that school. I became an *insider-outsider* and at other times an *outsider-insider*. As an *insider-outsider*, I was navigating a leadership role (part-time) while undertaking other educator roles outside of my school. The school role provided me with an intimate knowledge of my school's culture, history and dynamics, while work outside of the school could bring an outsider's perspective. This was valuable because working in different contexts meant that I could bring a fresh perspective to implementation issues, while also understanding the nuances of the organisation. When I was the 'outsider' and working in other school contexts, it gave me multiple opportunities to learn from others, but also share what I had learned in my own context. We could collectively adapt, adopt or adjust what we had learned from each other and our school contexts.

A generic strategy or solution cannot be applied to every situation. A one-size-fits-all approach fails to consider the nuances of each situation and can lead to solutions that are not effective – even if the research says it should be! School-improvement approaches should be tailored to address a school's contextual needs. I am an education practitioner who values working in varied school contexts with educators as they research, design and implement reform agendas that build sustainable practices over time. My focus remains on improved outcomes for *all* students. I understand schools are complex environments requiring flexible and collaborative approaches to achieve improved outcomes for those they serve.

Collaborative interactions can be powerful and, at the same time, problematic to accomplish. This is especially true when balancing multiple, and sometimes competing, demands within limited time frames. However, it is my belief that relationships are foundational to this work and have significant importance in the role they play for successful implementation of school-improvement initiatives.

Invitation to reconsider how we view silos and silo mentality

I have always been intrigued with the use of silos as a metaphor in organisations. The first reference to silos as a metaphor in organisational behaviour is believed to have been in 1987, when it was used to represent the idea of individual parts working together but independently, which is often the case in organisations. Silos are a useful metaphor to describe the lack of collaboration between departments that can arise in organisations, and the resulting lack of communication and exchange of ideas.

They can also be used to describe the difficulty of making organisational changes, as departments can be resistant to change and lack the resources necessary to make it happen or keep resources safely tucked away for themselves.

More recently, a definition adapted from Fox (2010) and Tett (2016) has given me cause for more thought in this area. Silos are a cultural phenomenon that result in psychological and physical barriers, which arise out of our human need to classify and organise our mental and social models. They provide us with the structure to cope with what can be seen to be chaos when working in complex organisations. However, silos and, more specifically, silo mentality, are seen as a form of organisational dysfunction and therefore the reason why every attempt is made to minimise or eradicate them. Interestingly enough, silos continue to exist within all types of organisations today, irrespective, or despite, the tools we have available to share information and the availability of wide-ranging skills, knowledge mobility and learning. It is why collaboration is a key strategy used to address the negative effects of silo mentality.

Looking more closely at schools, it is evident that historically there has been an 'egg carton' approach to the way schools can be organised. Working collaboratively necessitates significant changes to historical schooling practices that alter the way people relate to each other in and across schools. It requires school leaders and teachers to question existing organisational structures. Herein lies the paradox: collaboration is viewed as an essential component for school-improvement agendas and can mitigate isolation and silo mentality. Yet at the same time, collaboration within traditional school contexts can promote the same issue. This is because more is not always better.

Social brain theory (Dunbar, 1998) suggests that there may be optimal sizes and structures for organisations – including schools. The larger the school, the more relationships there are to manage. This then places certain limitations on individuals in maintaining these relationships. Maintenance is dependent on the frequency of interactions and a level of 'emotional closeness'. In this case, emotional closeness is determined on mutual and reciprocal trust. Given that we usually quantify relationships that take place in schools collectively – one teacher one class or one teacher two teams… you get the idea – we can underestimate the number of relationships trying to be maintained. In addition, think about the expectations for professional standards and principal profiles… over time, there has been a move to 'collective' responsibility for *all* students. We can very quickly reach the magical 150 relationships that Dunbar suggests as limited by cognitive capacity and time afforded to them.

While we can argue that each of these relationships is not expected to be strong, we do know that relationships are fundamental to the work being undertaken in schools. I would argue that as the educational landscape has changed, so too has the sophistication of the collaborative interactions to support student achievement – in all its forms. It is no wonder that silo mentality exists in our schools or organisations... it can act as a protective mechanism against cognitive and social overload.

Transferability

School improvement and associated frameworks often have limited shelf lives along with their related reform efforts – usually being pushed aside for the next cab off the rank. This lack of durability can often mean that initiatives are not fully implemented or are abandoned mid-stream because of changes in leadership, or a lack of deep understanding or even a belief in the initiative itself. Enhancing school-improvement viability requires a more realistic understanding of contextual organisational structures and the school culture in which the reform is to be implemented. At the same time, a quantitative measurement culture currently permeates research studies interrogating school-improvement strategies. This can be at the expense of important insights that could be discovered through qualitative approaches in evaluating implementation and impact.

While the research that forms the basis of this work was undertaken in secondary school contexts, I urge you to reflect on your own contexts and adapt, adjust or adopt key ideas and processes with the underlying principles in mind. Conversations with primary school colleagues assure me that this is as relevant for them as it is for their secondary counterparts.

Conclusion

This introductory chapter frames the purpose for engaging with this book and how each chapter is designed. It foregrounds my values and beliefs as an educator in attempts to make transparent what has shaped (or misshaped) key ideas and concepts that reflect the importance I see in the use of social brain theory to provide school leaders with a new lens to confront school-improvement issues. School leaders, in considering the nature of the relationship between human cognition and sociality, from an evolutionary point of view, can explore ways to address problems of practice that are based *on their own context*, rather than a one-size-fits-all approach.

While each chapter extends on concepts and ideas from previous chapters, these notions are reiterated and revisited throughout the book. Connecting and reminding you to use your context as the basis for mapping your next steps, educators from all levels of the organisation are being implored to balance the need for collaborative interactions with organisational structures that take into account the multiple demands of educators' work today. More specifically, this book invites you to consider that *individuals exhibit a finite communication capacity, which limits the number of relationships they can actively maintain at any one time*. If this is ignored as a factor contributing to the change process, then time, attention and cognitive constraints are not actively managed in the school-improvement process. *Addressing these constraints matters!* As leaders, you will note that progress towards long-term goals can be side-tracked, and collaboration viewed as a 'side order' to the 'real work'. As teachers, you will continue to drown in a sea of blah or be buffeted by the various demands that require your attention at any one time.

If what is being shared – so far – has resonated for you, then read on! Chapter 1 presents the *conceptual framework* that applies the existence of associations among structures that promote silo mentality, cognitive constraints for human interactions (social brain theory), collaboration as a strategy for improvement and leadership within school contexts. It considers that *social cognition, in brain evolution,* is unusually cognitively demanding. It is imperative that consideration be given to this when lamenting the so-called failures of collaboration for school improvement in school contexts.

Chapter 1

Leading with the Social Brain in Mind

New to me
- What is Leading with the Social Brain in Mind framework?
- How can school leaders strategically lead collaboration if there are cognitive limitations to interactions?

Revisiting, reviewing and revising familiar ideas
- Which aspects of social brain theory impacts the work we do?
- What processes have we put in place that might need to be strengthened or revisited? Why?
- How will these processes support students/staff that I work with?

Applying in unfamiliar, different or alternative contexts
- Which aspects of Leading with the Social Brain in Mind framework can I adapt, modify or adopt for our context?
- Why have I chosen these aspects to adapt, modify or adopt?
- How will I go about implementation?

Before you begin

Prior to reading this chapter, I invite you to reflect on your own knowledge (skills and experience) and thoughts (including values and beliefs) about what you already know about the social and cognitive complexity of collaboration. What you identify will support you in framing your 'take aways' from this chapter and, more importantly, how you decide on, and distinguish, the actions for your next steps.

Provocation

Does this resonate for you or members of your staff?

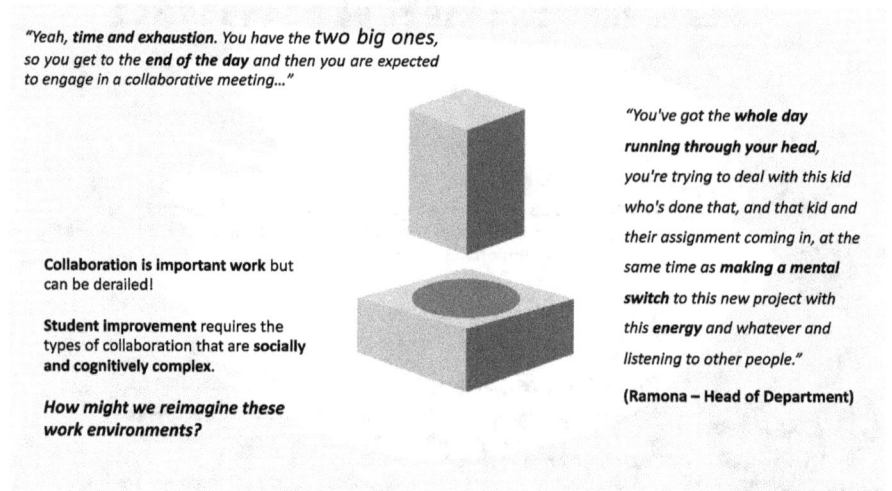

"Yeah, **time and exhaustion**. You have the **two big ones**, so you get to the **end of the day** and then you are expected to engage in a collaborative meeting..."

Collaboration is important work but can be derailed!

Student improvement requires the types of collaboration that are **socially and cognitively complex.**

How might we reimagine these work environments?

"You've got the **whole day running through your head**, you're trying to deal with this kid who's done that, and that kid and their assignment coming in, at the same time as **making a mental switch** to this new project with this **energy** and whatever and listening to other people."

(Ramona – Head of Department)

Questions to ponder

- Do you or others you work with experience cognitive fatigue?
- What does this look like, feel like and sound like in your school context?

Leading with the Social Brain in Mind framework

Educators are familiar with the use of frameworks that provide structure for planning and decision-making. These tools work more effectively when based on the best available data, rather than on instinct or opinion. Frameworks can also help leaders to better communicate and explore ideas with their teams. Decision-making as a consequence of employing a framework supports leaders in their efforts to ensure that available resources are used efficiently. Leading with the Social Brain in Mind is a framework that applies the existence of associations among organisational structures that are employed in schools to manage large groups of people (for example, departments, teams, year levels) and cognitive constraints for human interactions (social brain theory).

A framework for Leading with the Social Brain in Mind

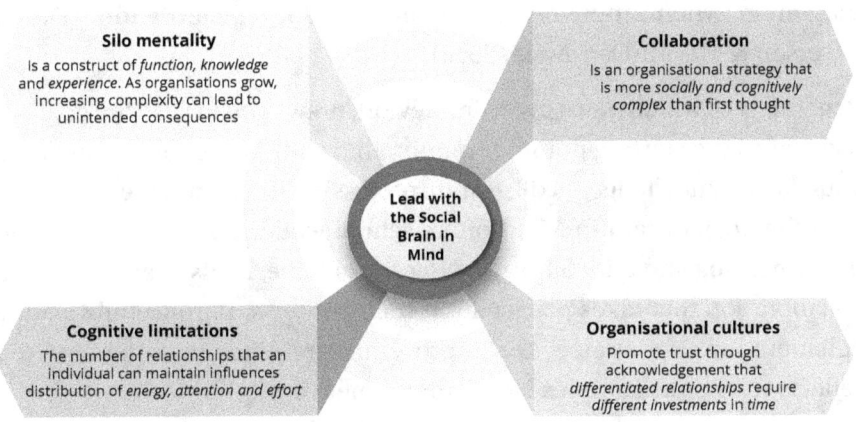

Silo mentality
Is a construct of *function, knowledge* and *experience*. As organisations grow, increasing complexity can lead to unintended consequences

Collaboration
Is an organisational strategy that is more *socially and cognitively complex* than first thought

Lead with the Social Brain in Mind

Cognitive limitations
The number of relationships that an individual can maintain influences distribution of *energy, attention and effort*

Organisational cultures
Promote trust through acknowledgement that *differentiated relationships* require *different investments* in time

If you were to close your eyes and think about the schools you have worked in, visited or seen in the media, then you might recognise similarities among their organisational structures – for example, year levels, subject departments or faculties – despite where they are located. Irrespective of the education system, schools are identifiable by certain organisational structures, and these have mostly remained consistent throughout history. They might be known by other names but essentially, they have the same function – to delineate by age and/or subject. For many, including the wider community, it can be difficult to imagine schools being organised in any other way. It is almost like they are entrenched in the DNA of schooling. *But* – these departmental structures can promote silo mentality.

Recognition of these insular behaviours has led to the use of collaboration as a whole-school strategy for improvement. The tensions that this creates for leaders have largely been ignored by policy. School leaders are left to problem solve – often with little support – the competing demands and expectations for increased collaboration in their school contexts. The research that underpins the framework discussed in this chapter acknowledges that social cognition, in brain evolution, is unusually cognitively demanding (Lewis et al., 2017) and when applied to school settings, the everyday work of educators is being underestimated within current organisational ways of working. Using the framework as a lens for reflection, exploration and dialogue, system and school leaders can begin to think in different ways about the inherent complexity and challenges that arise when implementing structures for collaboration (Drago-Severson & Maslin-Ostrowski, 2018).

Regardless of which piece of the framework draws you in first, the goal is to use that as the starting point for inquiry into your own context (including your own knowledge, skills and professional experience). Leading with the Social Brain in Mind offers school leaders ways to think about implementing and critically reviewing sustainable, realistic and impactful collaboration that takes place within their contexts. Purposefully leading collaboration as a strategy for improvement requires intentionality that reflects schools as complex work environments.

Collaboration is important work

Collaboration is highly regarded as a way of working in schools. As a strategy for improvement, it is employed as a vehicle to improve student learning outcomes and strengthen individual and collective teacher capacity (Australian Institute for Teaching and School Leadership, 2014; Sharratt, 2019). When collaboration is at its best there is an environment created with a shared vision and expectations for teaching and learning, whereby teachers can begin to close the gap between what is intended curriculum, what is implemented and what is attained by students (Marzano et al., 2005). Yet, the reality is not that simple.

Collaboration is an investment – a mammoth one! To devise organisational structures that provide opportunities for teachers to work together meaningfully about issues of teaching and student learning requires leaders to be economically, organisationally, structurally, professionally and personally agile. This is not to say that collaboration should be abandoned – far from it! We need to contextualise collaboration in relation to current research about the social and cognitive complexity of the work being undertaken in schools and then use this to reflect on the practices in place. More importantly, explore possibilities for reimagining the way we do things around here!

The benefits of collaboration are well documented in education literature and particular attention is drawn to issues of teachers working in isolation. Bringing teaching teams together to collaborate is intended to break down a siloed mentality and replace it with collective responsibility. However, without realising it, leaders could be perpetuating a collection of silos that are located side by side, with very little interaction among the different people within the 'silos'. Particularly, if over time the school grows in size and there are either multiple staffroom spaces or, worse, none, as space is no longer available! Consider the location of school buildings. For some staff it is easier to remain in their classroom, or building area, than it is to go to the staffroom located elsewhere.

When these examples are combined with the more 'compartmentalised' way that schools traditionally operate (timetables, year levels, subjects), then it is not surprising that although collaboration is intended school-wide to develop a shared vision, it can still be fragmented. Now, before you race off to reconfigure your school, it is important to understand that silos are not all bad (more about that in Chapter 5). We need to remember that in the fast-paced day-to-day operations of schools, feelings of frustration can be the right leverage to challenge long-held assumptions, beliefs, expectations and habits – particularly around those of collaboration.

Within the literature on collaboration there appears to be an underlying assumption that collaboration is more cost-effective than the effects of silo mentality (Andrews & Rapp, 2015; Department of Education and Training, 2018; Ford & Youngs, 2017). That is, the professional isolation and its associated effects cost an organisation more in terms of social capital than the unintended consequences and challenges associated with collaboration in school settings. Knowledge, strategy, time, energy and financial resources are required to implement collaboration within an organisation, and so not all forms of collaboration are equally strong, advantageous or have the desired effect (Hargreaves, 2019). So, despite the benefits, collaborative interactions can also have clear costs. Let me be clear – I am *not* saying we should give up on collaboration in schools! What I am saying is that we need to consider what else might be at play *when collaboration is not working in the ways that we believe it should.*

Leading with the Social Brain in Mind is a result of a study born out of curiosity for why something (collaboration) that appeared to be, for all intents and purposes, a 'silver bullet' – and it just makes sense – was becoming viewed as competition for limited resources and just too hard to sustain or maintain. *Collaboration on the run* became a phrase I heard all too frequently when speaking to colleagues in schools. Time was the number one barrier to collaborating with fidelity. Initially, I had some ideas why I thought this was the case, but it was reading Gillian Tett's book *The Silo Effect* (2016) that sent me in a direction that really gave me pause for thought. Although I inhaled every chapter as it unfolded, my mind buzzing with questions, it was the section on Dunbar's number that held me captive. I was entranced. Dunbar's number – social brain theory – provided some key elements to consider when thinking about collaboration in school settings.

Social brain theory (Dunbar's number)

Social brain theory refers to a quantitative relationship between social group size (number) and neocortex volume (Dunbar, 1998). It proposes that the principal selection pressure acting on the evolution of brains has been the cognitive demands of sociality (Dunbar, 2010). The relationship between neocortex volume and social group size, in studies undertaken by Dunbar and others (Dunbar, 2003, 2010; Dunbar & Shultz, 2007; Sutcliffe et al., 2018; Sutcliffe et al., 2012) suggests that the brain's computational capacity sets a limit on the number of individuals who can be held together in a coherent social group. This relationship predicts a group size of approximately 150 for humans at any given time and appears to be the typical size of both social communities in small-scale societies and personal social networks in the modern world (Dunbar, 1998, 2014a, 2014b). This includes online environments, but more on that later.

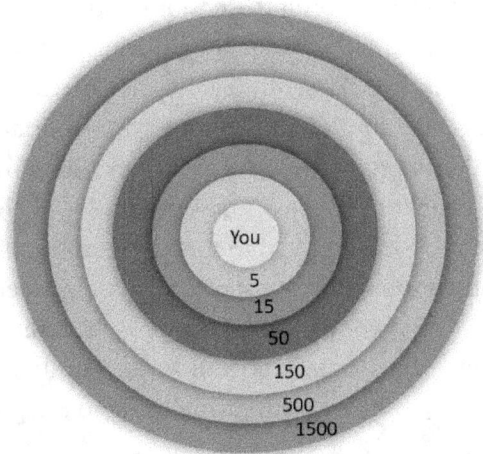

An individual (ego) sits within a series of hierarchically inclusive circles, or layers, of relationships that have a very distinct scaling ratio (each layer is three times the size of the one inside it). The heavy line demarcates the 150 layer, the typical size of personal social networks. Beyond this are acquaintances (500 layer); the layer at 1500 appears to represent the limit on the number of faces we can put names to. Frequency of contact, rated emotional closeness and willingness to act altruistically towards a given alter all decline across the successive circles (adapted from Dunbar, 2018, p36).

Just to reiterate... what is being said here is that the 'typical' human personal social network contains about 150 relationships including kin, friends and acquaintances (work colleagues, too), organised into a set of "hierarchically inclusive layers of increasing size but decreasing emotional intensity" (Tamarit et al., 2018, p8316).

Before moving on, please take a moment to think about a teacher who has multiple classes or multiple year levels or multiple subjects. Now, do the math and count the number of individuals that individual teacher would be collaborating with across a 'typical' week. Remember to include the number of individuals in each Teaching Team, Heads of Department, Deputy Principals, specialists and parents of students... You can see very quickly that numbers can exceed the 150 proposed by Dunbar.

In a study with secondary school educators, from varying positional roles and school systems (Government, Catholic and Independent), collaborative interactions averaged 177.22 across a week. Although this study occurred in a secondary school context, I would ask you to contemplate what this might look like in a primary context. For example, a primary teacher has one class, but teaches five to six subjects (or more) and possibly works within a team. Although a secondary teacher might only see their students two to three times a week (70 minutes per lesson), a primary school teacher (FTE) can potentially see their students every day for most of the school day. Add to this the number of parents/carers, specialists and other roles that are necessary for a teacher's day-to-day work and the collaborative interactions quickly mount up! Think about a specialist teacher in a primary school – the number of collaborative interactions across a week can be overwhelming to imagine.

To illustrate this, I have included the diagram that describes the findings in the study that underpins this book. Participants were asked to identify the number of interactions that took place for them with 11 specific positional roles as listed below:

Abbreviation	*Meaning*
CST	Cross-subject teams (not including year level team)
DP/AP	Deputy/Assistant Principal/s
EP	Executive Principal
HoD	Head of Department/s
OT	Other teams that I belong to (for example, data team, literacy team)
P	Principal
IC	Pedagogical/Instructional Coach
PoS	Parents of students I teach
SIT	Students that I teach or have direct responsibility for
TT	Teaching Team (year level/faculty)
Others	Other individuals not listed in the above categories

Here, Dunbar's hierarchically inclusive circles are used to illustrate an individual's number of interactions with positional roles (weekly).

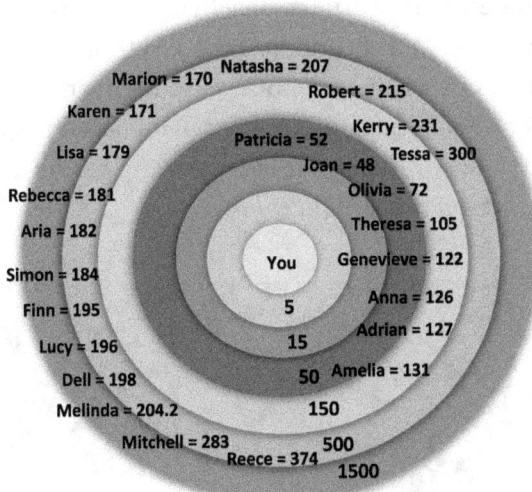

Energy, attention and effort are given to those individuals we determine closest and are the reason why networks are described as layered. With each increasing layer, emotional connectedness decreases, thus illustrating a correlation between the size of social networks and individuals' mentalising abilities (Dunbar et al., 2015; Mac Carron et al., 2016) – in other words, an individual's ability to understand another individual's beliefs about the world. This ability is referred to as *Theory of Mind* (Saxe, 2006; Wimmer & Perner, 1983) and in many adults, the limit to this ability is about five belief states, simultaneously, at any one time (four others plus your own). Think about the last social function you attended. Did you notice that groups were about four to five in number and if they happened to be larger, people tended to 'hang' together in smaller numbers? It is also why some researchers (Sih et al., 2009) believe that within a social group, differences among individuals in their social experiences and connections affect individual and group outcomes.

If we are to think of this in terms of the collaboration that takes place in schools, then we might begin to recognise why authentic collaboration takes time and energy. For example, the type of collaboration that occurs in schools to support student improvement is underpinned by several values and beliefs about learning and the learner (DuFour et al., 2017; Fullan & Quinn, 2016; Sharratt, 2018, 2019; Sharratt & Planche, 2018).

This can be students as learners, teachers as learners or leaders as learners. For instance, in a secondary school setting, teachers within the same department, or a primary school year level team, are collaborating on an assessment. Each person will be making attempts to understand each other's thinking – *I think that what you are saying is that we will... students will... and you think that I think...*

What this means is that each member of the team is involved in recursive understandings. These individuals are trying to 'mind read' the thinking behind the words and behaviours they are witnessing. A person's ability to balance separate mindstates of several individuals at the same time is complex and defined as higher-order intentionality (Lewis et al., 2017).

Collaboration, with a focus on student improvement, requires groups of individuals to understand each other's mindstate and intentions and as such, is cognitively taxing. More specifically, these conversations involve higher-order capacities that play a crucial role in an individual's ability to manage these conversations combined with what Beck (2017) describes as the intensification of workload associated with the teaching profession. The number of relationships matter!

Capitalising on social networks

Relationships are foundational for ALL work being undertaken in school contexts. The social structure, or the network of relationships among individuals, offers opportunities and constraints for the exchange of resources (Hargreaves, 2012; Vorhaus, 2014). Social capital, therefore, resides in the nature and quality of the relationships within an organisation rather than in the individuals themselves (Hargreaves, 2012; Jones & Harris, 2014). For this reason, collaboration is viewed as developing social capital and is dependent on the number and quality of the social relationships and embedded in the relationships among individuals, groups and networks (Andrews & Rapp, 2015; de Jong et al., 2016). However, if not understood or managed appropriately, its value may not be fully realised.

Leveraging social capital through collaboration, between teachers and school leaders around curriculum change and instructional excellence, provides a challenge. Apart from the logistics to make this happen, individuals do not weight each relationship equally and consequently distribute their energy, attention and effort to those individuals *they* determine as 'closest' (Dávid-Barrett & Dunbar, 2013; Dunbar, 2010; Tamarit et al., 2018). In this case, the individual defines this on the basis of frequency of contact and the trust they place in a perceived mutual and reciprocal relationship. It also contributes to how strong they perceive the relationship to be. In a school, this is influenced by the role or roles each individual is connected to. Teachers may distribute much of their energy, effort and attention to their students and teaching team, whereas a Deputy Principal may distribute more energy, effort and attention to teachers and Heads of Department. To give you an idea of how this might look, the diagrams on the next page are from participants from the study Leading with the Social Brain in Mind.

Remember that this is contextual and only meant to illustrate that the more you interact with certain, or groups of, individuals, the more time you are affording these relationships and not others. The important take away is that different relationships (social bonds) demand different *cognitive requisites and time investment.* Individuals distribute their social effort as a trade-off between costs and benefits that they attribute to the relationship. Psychologically, these trade-offs are related to the level of trust in a relationship, which is itself a function of the time invested in the relationship (Kolleck et al., 2021; Sutcliffe et al., 2012). The more time invested, the more likely trust can be reciprocated between individuals. However, we know that one does not automatically follow the other, but we do know that a key component of collaboration requires recognition that each person is working towards the good of improving student outcomes. This takes time to develop, because it is not an automatic given that we collectively understand what this means for each of us. We can assume that each of us carries the same 'picture' of curriculum, assessment, data, etc, in our heads, but we have different knowledge, experience and skills in these areas. Conversations where these might arise are time-consuming, and time is viewed as one of the main barriers to collaboration in schools.

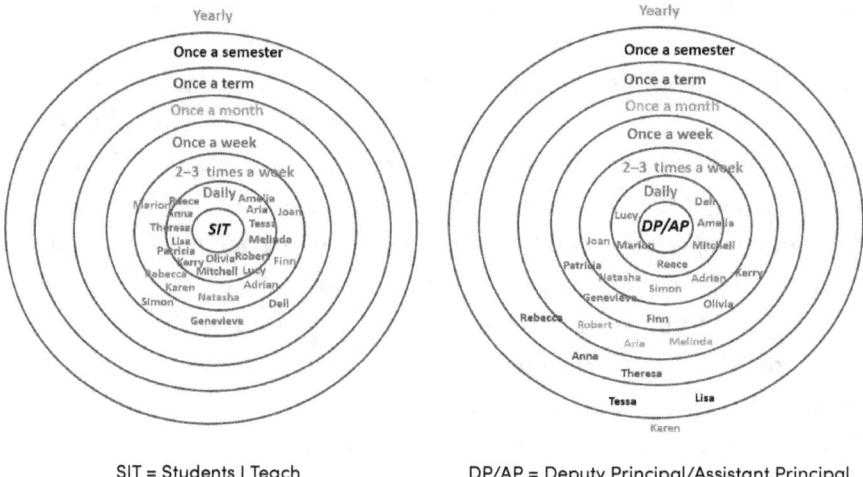

SIT = Students I Teach   DP/AP = Deputy Principal/Assistant Principal

What does this mean for schools?

Apart from the number of people that teachers are expected to interact with, collaboration also requires finding time in the workday – somewhere between teaching, planning tomorrow's lessons, marking yesterday's student papers to provide descriptive formative feedback, contacting parents or carers, making sure there is a record of contact for those discussions and possibly attending professional learning that aligns with their personal professional learning expectations. The changing and evolving nature of educators' work means that there are multiple demands vying for attention, often simultaneously, in the time available. It is not surprising then, that *this places cognitive constraints on individuals as they make the mental shifts to accomodate different types of relationships and associated tasks within limited time frames.*

To illustrate this, the social network below is an example of a group of individuals who have identifed the number of collaborative interactions they have with particular positional roles (students, parents, Teaching Teams, Heads of Department, Deputy Principal, Principal, Cross-subject Teams) across a week. Heavy traffic is clustered, not surprisingly, with students, Teaching Teams and Heads of Department.

Individual's interactions with positional roles network (weekly basis)

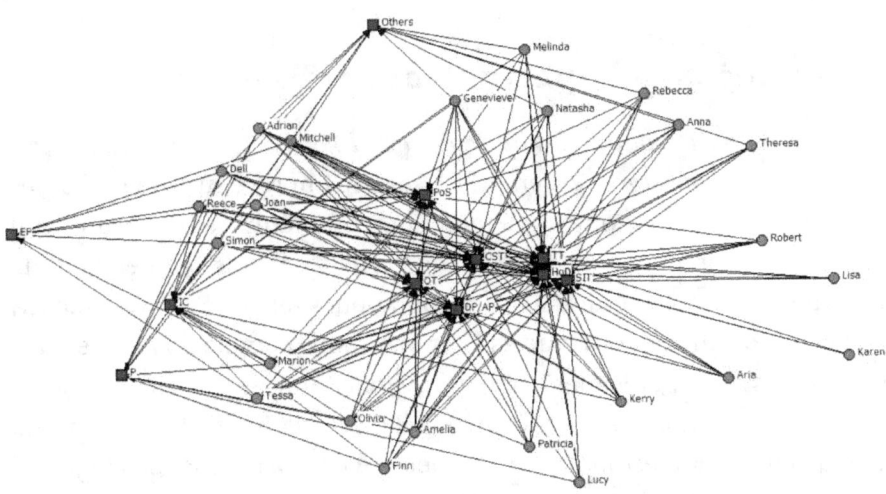

What is surprising is that Dunbar's layers suggest that the network owner has sets of relationships that progress in number of members but decreases in average emotional closeness and frequency of contact. However, it appears that school contexts may challenge this. For the individuals in this study, the number of identified collaborative interactions took place for the purpose of day-to-day work to support student improvement. At the same time, participants rated these collaborative relationships as strong.

What is important to recognise here is that in these complex multiple-task environments, an individual's performance depends critically on the interplay between cognitive control and cognitive capacity (Boag et al., 2019). Cognitive control is defined here as those processes that an individual uses to adapt, adjust and modify the cognitive system to meet specific task demands, and cognitive capacity describes a limited pool of cognitive resources involved in information processing (for example, attention, working memory) that can be allocated to various features of the task environment, but whose limited nature gives rise to resource congestion (Boag et al., 2019; Dávid-Barrett & Dunbar, 2016; Lewis et al., 2017; Tamarit et al., 2018). *It is reasonable to assume that for educators working in schools, the number of collaborative interactions is being underestimated in their cost to the individual and the hidden costs to the organisation.*

Apprenticing – important, but not sufficient

Leading schools requires additional and different types of knowledge, training and professional experience. Efforts to improve student outcomes have seen a focus on implementing continuous and meaningful collaborative interactions across and within schools. Understanding what it is and how to undertake collaboration is one thing, but in reality, collaboration in school contexts is much more complex. Not the least of which is a school leader's ability to create and design environments (Pont, 2020) that enable productive collaborative interactions to occur. We can often underestimate the number and type of interactions required for the types of collaboration taking place for capacity building and student improvement. Schools range in size and the larger a school is, the more likely it is that the average number of collaborative interactions for educators is more than 150 per week. This is because in schools we categorise relationships collectively (classes, teams, department). Consequently, the number of interactions can be miscalculated because they are 'lumped' together, rather than as independent interactions that take place.

Relationships cost. Maintaining each type of social bond demands different cognitive requisites and time investment. Time is limited in any organisation and schools are no exception. However, available time shapes and misshapes an individual's distribution of energy, attention and effort among the number of collaborative interactions necessary to undertake the professional expectations for educators. *Trying to maintain the number and types of relationships can have unintended consequences* (for the individual or team) that result in self-protective mechanisms. *Silo mentality* is one of these *self-protective mechanisms*.

If we are to capitalise on the benefits of collaboration in school contexts, then we also need to *provide leaders with additional and different types of knowledge, training and professional experience*. It is not sufficient to rely on an apprenticeship model that works with a 'luck of the draw' mentality and an assumption that all leaders are created equal. It also assumes that prior knowledge and experience is enough to lead, manage and innovate for change in today's educational landscape. I believe this is an excuse to abdicate responsibility for the necessary supports required of education systems and governments for school leaders to do the work expected of them.

Five Key Considerations

1. Change the language being used in your school from 'expenditure' to 'investment'. Operationalising the many components of a leader's role means the need to balance that time spent 'off campus' or in 'job-embedded' learning with overall costs to the individual and the organisation.
2. As a leader, be aware that you might be engaged in an *imagined past* that influences a *current imagined reality*. In other words, you might be using your past teaching/leading experiences to inform the work you are asking of your teachers/leaders, but not always understanding the day-to-day practicalities of these decisions.
3. Teaching loads matter. Remember cognitive capacity and cognitive control. For those individuals who have time available to them, they can *adjust the competing demands* to some degree, whereas those who have full-time teaching loads do not have this luxury.

4. Invest in time. Collaborative interactions are hindered by *unrealistic time-bound* expectations and deliverables that reflected perfunctory or symbolic efforts in addressing multiple agendas. Unfortunately, a leader's imagined reality *can underestimate* what can be accomplished in the time available.
5. Be aware and be proactive. Relying on your own initiative to seek the professional learning or skills that you require to lead may become an ad hoc approach – dependent on a range of factors (self-motivation, self-awareness, 'sink or swim'). Seek out and invite an *insider-outsider* to observe and provide feedback. A pair of neutral eyes may see what we are blind to!

Conclusion

The Leading with the Social Brain in Mind framework acknowledges that collaboration is important work in schools. However, it also recognises that the number and frequency of those interactions can take their toll on those engaged in the day-to-day work of teachers and leaders in service of supporting student improvement. The framework highlights that leaders can underestimate the time needed to invest in these collaborative interactions. Individuals distribute their energy, attention and effort unequally and determine this on the basis of frequency of contact and recognition of a mutual and reciprocal relationship.

Multiply and vying day-to-day demands shapes and misshapes this distribution of energy, effort and attention. Maintaining these relationships can have costs to the individual and the organisation in the form of silo mentality. Collaboration is cognitively taxing, and schools' organisational structures can add to the complexity of using collaboration as a whole-school improvement strategy. Without additional and different types of knowledge, training and professional experience, school leaders can be inadvertently contributing to further barriers to collaboration within their contexts. Employing the framework can support leaders in their investigations of what is working and what is not working in their contexts.

Mapping next steps

Use the self-check to see how many collaborative interactions you have in one typical week. Identify how many differentiated relationships there are. Audit your own staff to see how many collaborative interactions they undertake in one week. Remember, you can adjust the roles to suit your context.

Identify the number of people – within the categories below – that you have direct contact with throughout the course of a 'typical' school week.

Role	Number
Cross-subject teams (not including year level team)	
Deputy/Assistant Principal/s	
Executive Principal	
Head of Department/s	
Other teams that I belong to (for example, data team, literacy team)	
Principal	
Pedagogical/Instructional Coach	
Parents of students I teach	
Students that I teach or have direct responsibility for	
Teaching Team (year level/faculty)	
Other people in roles not included in the groups above	

1. Who are you currently collaborating with? Select which best describes the following: "I have been collaborating with this person/people on a regular basis (weekly) to…"

	Support student learning	Support my own professional learning	Support both (student learning and professional learning)	Not at all
Cross-subject teams				
Deputy/Assistant Principal/s				
Executive Principal				
Head of Department/s				
Other teams that I belong to (for example, data team, literacy team)				
Principal				
Pedagogical/Instructional Coach				
Parents of students I teach				
Students that I teach or have direct responsibility for				
Teaching Team				
Other people in roles not included in the groups above				

2. How often would you interact with this person/group?

	Every day	2–3 times a week	Once a week	Once a month	Once a term	Once a semester	Once a year
Cross-subject teams							
Deputy/Assistant Principal/s							
Executive Principal							
Head of Department/s							
Other teams that I belong to (for example, data team, literacy team)							
Principal							
Pedagogical/Instructional Coach							
Parents of students I teach							
Students that I teach or have direct responsibility for							
Teaching Team							
Other people in roles not included in the groups above							

3. Using the description/scale below and based on the previous responses, how would you describe the strength of the relationship?

	Very Strong: We have frequent and/or purposeful contact that has led to enduring, long-lasting connections	**Strong:** We have frequent (1–2 times a week) and/or purposeful contact	**Less Strong:** We have infrequent (1–2 times a term) and/or superficial contact	**Not Strong:** I hardly know this person, or I used to know them, but we no longer work together contact	**Not Applicable:** The person is new to the school or role
Cross-subject teams					
Deputy/Assistant Principal/s					
Executive Principal					
Head of Department/s					
Other teams that I belong to (for example, data team, literacy team)					
Principal					
Pedagogical/Instructional Coach					
Parents of students I teach					
Students that I teach or have direct responsibility for					
Teaching Team					
Other people in roles not included in the groups above					

Now that you have this data, read the next chapter to understand why the very strategy you are employing, *in the way that you are employing it*, could be contributing to silo mentality within your context.

Chapter 2

Schools as complex organisations

New to me
- Can I/we explain the difference between a complex and complicated organisation?
- Why are schools considered complex? What key features do they exhibit?
- What additional and different types of knowledge, training and professional experience is required to lead complex organisations (in this case, schools)?

Revisiting, reviewing and revising familiar ideas
- Which aspects of complexity theory would I/we like to explore further?
- What theories do I/we use or will choose to strengthen or revisit? Why?
- How will I/we recognise inherent gaps that come about through my/our use of these theories and practices?

Applying in unfamiliar, different or alternative contexts
- Which aspects of my knowledge can I/we adapt or modify to suit my/our context?
- Why have I/we chosen these aspects?
- What key ideas will I/we need to be mindful of as I/we go about implementation?

Before you begin

While we acknowledge that schools are *complex organisations* and can describe the effects on those working in schools, it's not often that leaders are given an opportunity to explore and then apply those theories that underpin complex organisations. This is because the *application of these theories* to schools is *relatively new* and there has been a shift in thinking about complexity from a *mechanistic view to a more organic view* of leading change. In this chapter, you are invited to consider what you already know (skills and experience) and what you think (including values and beliefs) about schools as complex organisations. Recognising these aspects will support you in framing your 'take aways' from this chapter and, more importantly, how you determine which actions will support you in your current or future work.

Provocation

> **Dianne (Classroom Teacher):** "We've had to fit so much into the meeting schedule that there hasn't been time to value that other kind of collaboration – within a year level. This is because we just can't manage all the other things. There are so many other pieces that we're required to do as part of being part of the school. There are different meeting groups and we need to work with our faculties. I would say that time [lack of it] and then also just the busyness of the school [gets in the way of collaboration]."

In what ways does organising collaboration to improve school outcomes feel like a high ropes course?

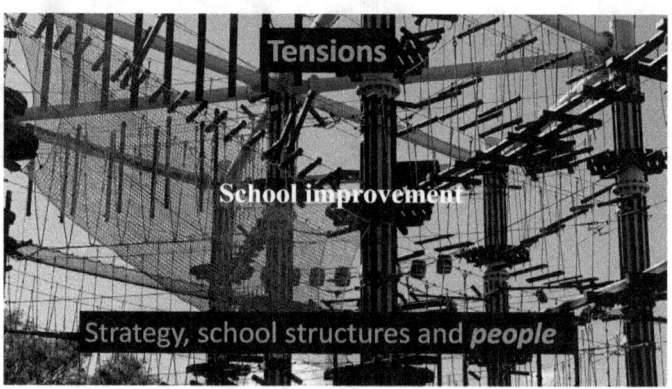

Questions to ponder

- As a leader, how do you organise structures for collaboration?
- What if the very structures you were employing were contributing to silo mentality?

Defining complex organisations

'Complex' is a common description used in relation to schools today. As with other concepts in education, we can toss them around and have a belief that members of our school community share a common understanding that will provide a consistency of approaches across the school. Unfortunately, this is not always the case. Researchers agree that 'complexity' is difficult to define and quantify, but for the purposes of your explorations in this chapter, we will define complex organisations as "complex systems comprised of dynamic networks of relationships" (Hogue & Lord, 2007, p373). Further, they are characterised by many different components and factors that interact with one another in interdependent ways. There are researchers who study the behaviours of these systems and are known as complexity theorists. They argue that no single organism exists in isolation and as such these researchers use various theoretical frameworks to understand and analyse how the different parts of an organisation interact with each other and how these interactions contribute to the overall behaviour of the organisation.

Complexity theory can support leaders in applying the characteristics of these organisations to their own contexts. What is important to know is that processes, relationships and interactions in complex organisations are often nonlinear, meaning that small changes in one part of the organisation can have large effects on the overall behaviour of the entire organisation. This is different to complicated systems. They can be completely described in terms of their individual components – even when there are large numbers of them. In complicated systems, the various parts are connected in a straightforward manner, while in complex systems, the various parts not only connect but also influence and are influenced by each other. The difference between a complex and complicated system is important for a school leader to understand because this knowledge can influence decisions related to the change process.

Some of the key features of complex organisations include:

- Exhibiting spontaneous instability that is unpredictable in nature (Devereux et al., 2020)
- Organisation structures that are used to divide tasks and responsibilities, and to ensure that decisions are made in an orderly and efficient manner
- A high degree of specialisation, with different employees or units focusing on specific tasks or areas of expertise
- Sets of rules and procedures in place to guide decision-making and the allocation of resources; this can help to ensure that the organisation runs smoothly, but it can also lead to bureaucracy and slow decision-making
- Multiple stakeholders that can make it challenging to balance the needs and interests of all these groups
- More complexity due to the nature of their size – the more employees and departments, the more likely they will have their own goals, objectives and ways of working
- Processes and procedures for efficiency that may not allow for flexibility and adaptability

One of the key insights of complexity theory is that it is often difficult to predict the behaviour of complex systems. This can make it challenging for organisations to anticipate and respond to changes in their environment. However, complexity theory also suggests that there may be patterns and regularities in the behaviour of complex systems that can be identified and used to better understand and manage these systems. Overall, complexity theory provides a useful framework for understanding the dynamics of organisations and can be applied in a variety of contexts, including schools.

Complexity in schools

If we were to use the above characteristics as a checklist for determining schools as complex organisations, then it is not too long before we see that schools exhibit many (if not all) of these key features. In schools, however, it is the addition of the sheer volume of individuals a teacher or leader is required to interact with on a daily basis alongside the context of the work being undertaken that makes this different to other organisations. In this case, complexity is referred to as a 'layering' of multiple demands and expectations requiring numerous interactions, skills and processes being undertaken within limited time frames. Crucially, these 'layers' necessitate additional time and cognitive energy because working across different groups of people and switching cognitive resources to accommodate the tasks being undertaken uses higher-order intentionality (more on this in Chapter 3). Higher-order intentionality can be underestimated in schools!

Complexity is often raised as an issue for undertaking meaningful or authentic collaboration in schools. Although there can be many reasons for this, one (I believe) can be attributed to the very nature of schools – they are organised in predictable ways (timetables, terms) and yet on any one day there can be numerous 'events' that take place that are not planned or expected to occur. These occurrences are spontaneous and unpredictable. For example, a fire alarm going off during an assessment task can throw out all the previous planning for order and predictability. If we return to the key features of complex organisations, then we note that they display unpredictable behaviours. Yet, schools have worked in ways to create certainty through predictability. This is problematic for school leaders.

Current models of schools often reflect ingrained and historical practices that have remained unchanged or unchallenged for decades. Collaboration necessitates significant changes to previous schooling practices that alter the way people relate to each other in and across schools and require school leaders to consider the associations among their school-improvement strategy, their organisational structures and cognitive constraints being placed upon educators in their contexts. Complexity in schools acknowledges the belief that individuals exhibit a finite communication capacity, which limits the number of relationships they can actively maintain at any one time and as such should not be ignored as a factor contributing to the change process. A recent study illustrated that those educators, with various positional roles, were exceeding the 150 interactions. These weekly collaborative interactions are undertaken as part of the everyday work of teachers and leaders in school contexts with colleagues in various positional roles. This highlights that these interactions are not confined to specific roles within school contexts. The expectation for collaboration is for everyone, irrespective of your position.

Individual's number of interactions with positional roles (weekly)

Pseudonym	Role	CST	DP/AP	EP	HoD	OT	P	IC	PoS	SIT	TT	Others	Total
Mitchell	Executive Principal	4	4	4	20	4	10	2	12	10	13	200	283
Kerry	Classroom Teacher	5	3	0	3	2	0	2	1	200	15	0	231
Natasha	Classroom Teacher	10	3	0	3	3	0	2	1	155	20	10	207
Robert	Classroom Teacher	0	1	0	2	1	0	0	1	200	10	0	215
Lisa	Classroom Teacher	3	0	0	2	0	0	0	0	170	4	0	179
Theresa	Classroom Teacher	11	1	0	1	0	0	0	0	80	10	2	105
Melinda	Classroom Teacher	20	0	0	3	0	0	1	0.2	150	20	10	204.2
Tessa	Classroom Teacher	2	2	1	3	1	0	1	5	260	25	0	300
Anna	Head of Department Student/Staff	3	0	0	2	1	0	0	5	75	10	30	126
Karen	Classroom Teacher	0	0	0	1	0	0	0	0	150	20	0	171
Aria	Classroom Teacher	2	2	0	1	1	0	0	0	160	16	0	182
Lucy	Head of Department Curriculum	20	1	0	4	0	1	0	0	150	20	0	196
Rebecca	Head of Department Curriculum	0	1	0	1	2	0	0	5	150	20	2	181
Simon	Deputy Principal	15	5	1	10	30	1	2	10	80	10	20	184
Amelia	Head of Department Curriculum	8	1	0	10	7	1	1	15	70	18	0	131
Adrian	Head of Department Student/Staff	1	5	0	10	2	1	2	10	90	4	2	127
Reece	Head of Department Student/Staff	12	4	1	12	18	1	2	6	300	6	12	374
Patricia	Head of Department Curriculum	0	1	0	4	12	0	1	2	30	2	0	52
Olivia	Pedagogical Coach	6	1	0	6	3	1	1	1	50	3	0	72
Finn	Head of Department Curriculum	80	1	0	8	3	1	4	0	90	8	0	195
Genevieve	Head of Department Student/Staff	3	1	0	2	4	0	1	15	89	4	3	122
Marion	Secondary Campus Principal	3	1	1	30	4	4	4	1	108	14	0	170
Dell	Deputy Principal	5	5	1	10	10	1	2	8	70	6	80	198
Joan	Head of Department Student/Staff	5	1	4	8	2	1	1	1	18	2	5	48

It is clear from this example that there is an underestimation of the number of collaborative interactions required of these individuals in these schools. If you mapped the collaborative interactions in your own school (Chapter 1), how does this compare? If it is similar, then there are implications for how school leaders organise collaborative interactions – whatever their primary purpose. Unfortunately, relationships (historically) in schools have been described in a dyadic way – a teacher and their class, a Head of Department and their department, or a Principal and their school. Therefore, this assumes that the relationship is one-to-one, but this is not an accurate way to quantify the number of relationships for those individuals working in schools.

Quantifying relationships in this way dismisses the efforts necessary to maintain them for the work being undertaken to improve student outcomes. This does not take into account the learning that is occurring for teachers. Although not undertaken specifically for teachers, functional MRIs reveal patterns of activation within certain regions of the brain that have been interpreted as a neural network for managing multiple interpretations of others' mindstates (Lewis et al., 2017). In other words, in collaborative interactions individuals expend energy and effort in making attempts to make sense of what another person is saying and how they are acting. They reconcile (or not) these interpretations with their own thinking and experience. When time, attention and cognitive constraints are not actively managed in the school-improvement process, then progress towards long-term goals can be side-tracked with the strategy of collaboration viewed as an interference to what needs to be done.

More specifically, the lack of quantifying relationships in schools has ignored the complexity that this brings to school-improvement initiatives. When employing collaboration in school contexts, it is important that system and school leaders do not underestimate what it takes the individual to maintain these collaborative relationships. Ignorance is not bliss – it only exacerbates contributions to silo mentality as a self-protection mechanism for cognitive overload. Silos and silo mentality are not the enemy. They are a natural phenomenon that leaders can leverage when recognising signs and symptoms of complex organisations that contribute to siloed mentality.

Silos and complexity

Although Chapter 5 will discuss silo mentality more comprehensively, the relationship between complex organisations and silo mentality will be discussed here. Complex organisations and silos appear to be symbiotic within a school context. Being pulled in multiple directions and having to make multiple professional decisions (Beck, 2017) can bring about a sense, or feelings, of chaos. As a response, individuals or teams can develop silo mentality. Silos offer a framework for managing the chaos and provide a structure for dealing with the complexity. For individuals and the organisation, silos give us a way to handle the disorder in addition to a system for coping with the unpredictability. They offer a means of navigating the turmoil. For schools this can be challenging for improvement at a whole-school level, but it doesn't have to be this way.

Working with and understanding complex organisations in school contexts assists leaders in making sense of competing tensions. Unless leaders have experience or knowledge of alternative ways to navigate the issues that emerge when employing collaboration within traditional school organisational structures, then *complexity* contributes to a silo mentality on an organisational level. This is because the nature of *complexity is bounded* by the experience and knowledge of the individual (for example, seeing curriculum silos, silo in roles, but not necessarily other functions of the school such as timetabling, finance.) Without disruption to current experience, alternative or additional knowledge, leaders maintain the structures and ways of working that they currently know. To illustrate, collaborative interactions are hindered by unrealistic time-bound expectations and deliverables that reflect perfunctory or symbolic efforts in addressing multiple agendas. If you haven't already done so, make a list of the priorities you identify as supporting an improvement agenda in your school. Then ask five other people in the school to do the same. Make sure these individuals represent different positions or roles, including students. Compare the lists. What did you find? How many are there?

Each different priority identified represents a layer for individuals to manage in addition to their day-to-day work. Please note that I am not saying that you need to remove or reduce these, but there are ways to balance the expectations that surround them. The challenge for leaders is that they can experience a sense of urgency in *getting* the work done and *imagining* that multiple agendas can be undertaken simultaneously as they consider them as 'just part of the everyday work'. In reality, this is not the case for those undertaking the work on a day-to-day basis.

Kate (Head of Department): "There's just never a minute's downtime to think of stuff."

A leader's *imagined* reality can underestimate what can be accomplished in the time available. *Imagined* because it reflects a leader's past (teaching/leadership) experiences that are used to shape their decision-making processes. Specifically, when these experiences are used to inform the work teachers are undertaking, there can be a disparity with the intent and outcome of these decisions. I am *not* diminishing a leader's experience, but the further away we move from the day in and day out of classroom practice, the more likely we underestimate additional layers that result from an evolving workload. Comparing the day-to-day demands of working in schools today is not the same as 10 years ago, and teachers can feel that leaders forget or have not experienced some of the challenges they face today. Each social bond demands different cognitive requisites and time investment, particularly in face-to-face interactions. Less time available means less time to maintain each type of social bond required for different teams or individuals. This works in reverse for leaders, too. Teachers and those who may previously have had a leadership role are more likely to underestimate or hold misconceptions for the work being undertaken by leaders today. Again, this is a consequence of the types of work that leaders are expected to carry out in an evolving educational workspace. Leaders today require additional and different types of knowledge, training and professional experience.

> **Andrew (Classroom Teacher):** "I think the longer they're [school leaders] away from the classroom, the less... let's say, they remember, so to speak, and it's just natural... I've taught Year 7 for the first time, after [teaching Year 9] for three years... even then I just kind of rocked up [expecting to start teaching in the same way] and realised I had forgotten what Year 7 is like... the Principal of the college has been out of a classroom for 10 to 20 years... they don't remember... and teaching has changed since then."

A mismatch between theory and practice for those leading the work and those doing the work can unwittingly strengthen unhelpful narratives. To give you an idea, while a leader might believe they lead by example during meetings, teachers can view this type of interaction as interruption and as 'chewing' into valuable time that competes with day-to-day operations and time intended for deep discussions about teaching and learning. In other words, depending upon the positional role, competing tensions can eventuate. Each role intends for meeting schedules *to divide tasks and responsibilities, and to ensure that decisions are made in an orderly and efficient manner* and yet with a prevailing sense of urgency, often found in schools, meetings can be hijacked by other agendas that are important, but in competition with the available time, effort and attention already being distributed.

Disconnections and misconceptions

The roles and expectations for leading and teaching in schools has become more complex in past decades. Processes and procedures that have been supplemented with technology have produced efficiency from an organisational standpoint, but additional and time-consuming layers for the individual. These and other examples produce competing tensions that lead to disconnections and misconceptions (imagined past and current realities) that produce a lingering aftermath for those involved.

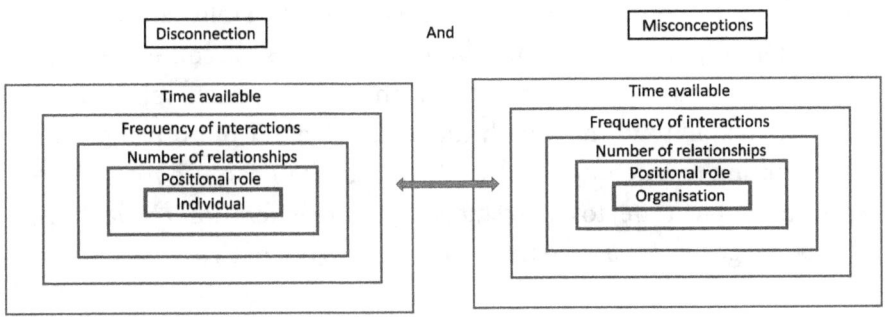

Disconnections come about as a consequence of a siloed mentality where the parts of the organisation are prioritised at the expense of the whole. The individual balances the number, frequency and purpose of collaborative relationships with their role (sometimes multiple roles) within the time available and, more often than not, within organisational structures that have not adapted to the changing nature of the work. As an example, a full-time teaching load as compared with a teaching load for a Head of Department, Deputy Principal or Principal amplifies competing tensions because their energy, effort and attention are being expended across multiple students at the same time but with little time to adjust or cognitively make the switch to the next piece of work.

Angela (Classroom Teacher): "Maybe because you [leaders] don't have the class face time that a teacher with a full load has. So, there's a bit more leeway in your day to go and seek someone out. I've got more spares [non-contact] than them [teachers]. I have more flexibility to meet with them. And I don't mind using my lunchtime to catch up with teachers because I can use my spare [non-contact time] to eat my lunch. While teachers don't have that advantage. So, it's a time thing to be able to do that."

Misconceptions about the organisation and the individuals within it are a result of worldviews that do not match current realities. Schools can be locked into particular ways of working because those that work within them cannot imagine another way of them working. Schools as complex organisations require leaders that can acknowledge uncertainty and *lean into behaviours, attitudes and dispositions* that interpret emerging events rather than direct events, encourage innovation rather than innovate, and manage words rather than manage people. This has implications for leadership preparation and the types of work leaders will do.

Leading as practitioners and as theorists

There are many types of leadership styles and descriptions. If you were to take 30 seconds to brainstorm all the ones you have heard, I imagine you would come up with at least five (if not more). What I am proposing here is not an additional one, but a refinement on those in existence. Precision in leadership practice requires school leaders to embrace evidence-informed research (Sharratt, 2019). Schools as complex organisations compel educators to interrogate theory *with* contextual practice. Issues arise when there is an inconsistent understanding of theory *and* practice, or when there are gaps in perceptions of the practical application of collaborative work in addtion to other day-to-day operational demands. From a leadership perspective, what is needed is someone who can recognise, foreground and act on those competing tensions that bring about disconnections and misconceptions.

Leaders who seek to understand competing tensions when leading collaboration as a strategy for school improvement are interactional practitioners *and* theorists. They use research to inform their knowledge base, but use their context to enable emergent futures by disrupting patterns through the use of conflict and uncertainty. At this point, please stay with me. I know this might seem counterintuitive if you have worked in schools for some time!

> **Daniel (Head of Department):** "I don't know what they call it – redefining? But it's not redefining, it's upgrading the level of work to be done on the level of expertise or skills necessary."

These types of leaders seek avenues to broaden different types of knowledge, skills sets and professional experience in recognition that their apprenticeship pathway to leadership has shaped and misshaped their worldviews in specific ways. This means, as leaders, they actively invest in interactional practice to redefine and refine their work as theorists. Interactional practice recognises that the cognitive demands of sociality have been underestimated in schools and thus need to be proactively addressed when employing collaboration as a strategy for improvement. In other words, leaders are doing all they can to redress imagined past realities with imagined current realities for individuals and the teams they work with. Theories for why collaboration is or is not working can be challenged or affirmed by stronger understandings of the practices occurring, not what they imagine is, or 'should be', occurring. Therefore, Leading with the Social Brain in Mind, as interactional practitioners, and theorists, means working from an understanding that those competing tensions based in imagined past realities can shape and misshape imagined current realities for individuals and the organisation.

When leaders investigate how to effectively promote collaboration in school settings, and explore potential barriers to communication, such as cognitive limitations, they must adapt their approach to suit the specific context they are working in. As a result, they become more attuned to the nuances and complexities of that particular environment. In effect, they are testing their theories about problems of practice in their school contexts. That is, they examine the disconnection among the aspects for individuals and how they contribute to the misconceptions for their school (the organisation as a whole). Leading as interactional practitioners and as theorists reduces the inherent gaps that come about with imagined realities.

Apprenticing – important but not sufficient

Leading schools requires additional and different types of knowledge, training and professional experience.

> **Angela (Classroom Teacher):** "I think that might be the same for a lot of Heads of Department, unless they've acted in it before. There is no training. Like it's just – here you go… run with it. Do what you want with it. Here are some guidelines, but there you go. That's hard! You get trained to be a teacher; you get prac in a classroom with the supervisor. You get dropped into the pool, learn on the run and it is sink or swim."

The changing nature of the job and how it has increased in complexity requires leaders to operationalise the many components of their roles, in addition to knowing what implications this has for school improvement in a highly collaborative environment. A complex system, such as a school, requires leaders to enact less 'mechanistic' views that enable them to lead "spontaneous instability that can occur within complex systems" (Devereux et al., 2020, p415). Strategic leadership takes on another dimension in a complex organisation such as a school. Unpacking the assumptions that are operating within the school is important. Assumed understandings can create those inherent gaps for individuals and teams. I would suggest that explorations around causal relationships would be a good place to start. You know the ones I mean... if we do this, then we will get this result or outcome. The next one to look at are time frames to achieve the outcomes and results you are expecting. Usually, time frames are bound by a school calendar year and are not realistic or reasonable in the time available.

Leaders investing in their own learning is a necessity, not an option. This is a balancing act and one where leaders can too often reject this investment because it does not seem cost-effective. Calculating the overall costs to the individual and the organisation can often mean a leader will choose to forego learning that can be beneficial.

> **Sarah (Head of Department):** "Learning on the job makes it that much more complex as well, because you're dealing with new processes that you may not have been aware of. And you don't know what's required behind those processes. So, you've got to go to the PDs, which means you are off campus, you're out of touch, and it's just time and money again."

Leadership capabilities for schools are yet to actively address schools as complex organisations. More specifically, leaders can be unaware that the very structures they employ for collaborative interactions can be promoting silo mentality. Leading with the Social Brain in Mind inevitably challenges worldviews about historical structures like 'timetables' and 'teaching loads' that are employed as an efficient, practical way for schools to operate when managing large numbers of people; assigning accountabilities, responsibilities and bringing a sense of predictability and order does not occur without intention. These entrenched practices add to the frustrations of designing collaboration within complex organisations. Staffing models need to be reimagined to make the best use of the resources available. At the same time, it means that leaders need to understand that silo mentality is a naturally occurring phenomenon that shares characteristics that can be both advantageous and problematic for individuals and organisations. Therefore, it is essential that school leaders today are able to recognise when excessively insular mindsets or mentality, including their own, shape and misshape behaviours and ways of working that inhibit collaboration as a strategy for school improvement.

Valerie (Campus Principal): "It's [skill and knowledge building] left to the schools, to the people on the ground in the schools. ... you've got to hope that you've got talented senior officers who are able to do that – who are able to work that into their daily operations."

Leaders use what is familiar to them in leading the work – their own experience and knowledge. Think about how collaborative interactions take place in your context. Does it look anything like the following?

1. **Using designated meeting times after the workday has concluded**
   After work means that teachers may not be fully in the present or are too tired to engage in the mentalising required for collaborative interactions to improve student outcomes.

2. **Utilising a student-free day**
   Using a student-free day means waiting lengthy periods between collaborations, risking other demands take precedence and focus for interactions lost over time.

3. **What might appear to be a better alternative – teams being released during the workday can create different issues**
   For example, teachers would argue that there is twice the amount of work needed to be released to collaborate with their colleagues – preparation for their classes on the day of release and then the work on the day. School leaders would suggest that large teams being replaced is a financial cost in addition to behavioural problems that eventuate with such a large change to routine for students.

   Simon (Deputy Principal): "...it almost takes a little bit of detraining, in terms of people operating in a way that they know is in their mind efficient and delivers some results."

If we continue to use an apprenticeship-based model (I am not saying we should abandon it!), then system leaders need to examine the types of knowledge that leading schools with collaborative interactions are at the foundation for what they do. One only has to look at the *Australian Professional Standard for Principals and the Leadership Profiles* to know that additional and different types of knowledge, training and professional experience goes beyond their learning in their *teacher* education courses.

There is an expectation...

Australian Professional Standard for Principals and the Leadership Profiles

Principals network and **collaborate** *with a wide range of people* to secure the best possible learning outcomes and wellbeing of all students

Principals can communicate, negotiate, **collaborate** and advocate effectively and relate well to all in the school's community

They seek to build a successful school through effective **collaboration** with school boards, governing bodies, parents and others

They also assess their own and the school's effectiveness, and work to build networks, **collaborate** with educational groups and make connections beyond their own school

Effective leadership is distributed and **collaborative**, with teams led by the Principal working together to accomplish the vision and aims of the school

Principals also define challenges clearly and seek positive solutions, often in **collaboration** with others

Leading a complex organisation involves the following:

Types of knowledge

- Exploring attributes of complex organisations and implications for leading schools.
- Nonlinear sequences and unpredictability are an expectation not the exception (what does this mean for organisational structures?).
- Beliefs about causal relationships need to be reviewed (what does this mean for evidence- and data-informed decisions?).
- Complexity versus chaotic.
- Certainty versus adaptive systems.
- The work in schools is *ever evolving*.
- Conflict is a normal manifestation of differentiated interests (resistance and dissent is useful for recognising silos *and* a way to capitalise on innovative possibilities).
- Communication requires investments in time, effort and energy (how do the communication processes currently in use add complexity to the work being undertaken?).
- Complex organisations *will not* have everyone on the same page, at the same time.

Professional experience

- Recognition of push-pull scenarios between opposing forces. Discussions that explore how these enact a social reality for different groups.
- Co-construction *with* peers to develop contingencies and possibilities rather than linear sequences.
- Relational processes are an investment that is contextual. Build context experiences to share and compare with networked experiences.
- Communication as dialogue.

Skills

- Relational and interactional – those communication skills that will develop widespread agreement in a collective on overall goals, aims and mission.
- Emotional intelligence – communication skills that work towards alignment of the organisation and coordination of knowledge and work in a collective.
- Social intelligence – commitment and a willingness of individuals to work in interests of the school as community.
- Cultural intelligence – trust for the organisation and people within it is an ongoing process that is *actively* built over time and based on actions and words of all.

Conclusion

Complex organisations exhibit spontaneous instability that is unpredictable in nature (Devereux et al., 2020). Yet schools are organised in predictable ways (for example, timetables, terms). Complexity in schools is referred to as a 'layering' of multiple demands and expectations requiring numerous interactions, skills and processes being undertaken within limited time frames and using additional time and cognitive energy. Being pulled in multiple directions and having to make multiple professional decisions (Beck, 2017) can bring about a sense, or feelings, of chaos. As a response, individuals or teams can develop silo mentality.

Silos provide the structure to cope with the chaos (Tett, 2016). It is the natural order of complex organisations to experience competing tensions, and these can lead to disconnections and misconceptions (imagined past and current realities) that produce a lingering aftermath. Leading as practitioners and as theorists reduces the inherent gaps that come about with imagined realities. *Leading schools requires additional and different types of knowledge, training and professional experience.*

Mapping next steps

Dedicate time to check in and see what assumptions are at play for individuals about the following:

- Purpose for key initiatives
- Importance of key initiatives in relation to their team/ sub school/faculty
- Length of time it takes to develop components of curriculum/ initiatives
- When and where collaboration takes place
- Definitions of terms and key initiatives
- Why do certain organisational structures exist?
- Purpose of meetings
- Do meetings fulfil their purpose in the time available?

What are the competing tensions in your context? What are your top three?

Use the example overleaf to see if aspects resonate for you or your team. Self-reflect on one to explore further. What self-learning would you like to invest in?

Competing tensions can lead to disconnection and misconceptions

Disconnection	Misconceptions
• Silo mentality – prioritising the parts at the expense of the whole. • Cognitive overload – underestimating demands of sociality when collaborating for school improvement. • Retreating as self-protection from cognitive demands. • Structures that do not adapt to the changing nature of the work. • Organisations are locked into particular historical ways of working. • Perceptions of support offered and required by different roles. • Perceptions of the work for and by different roles.	• Apprenticing is sufficient for school leaders for education today. • Changing nature of the work. • History necessitates organisations are locked into particular ways of working. • Being all on the same page at the same time. • Using the jargon means authentic implementation. • Urgency to get the work done means it is being done with fidelity.

Now that you are familiar with the key characteristics of a complex organisation and the skill sets that support your leadership of them, read Chapter 3 to strengthen your commitment to collaboration as a strategy. In this next chapter you will discover how you can influence the socially and cognitively complex aspects of collaboration that have previously gone unrecognised.

Chapter 3
Collaboration is socially and cognitively more complex than first thought

New to me
- Can I/we explain why collaboration is socially and cognitively complex?
- What hidden costs to collaboration can be found in your school context?
- What additional and different types of knowledge, training and professional experience is required to lead collaboration?

Revisiting, reviewing and revising familiar ideas
- Which aspects of collaboration in our school context would I/we like to explore further?
- What do I/we do to support our teams in their development of higher-order capacities to manage conversations that require understanding of another person's mindstate and intention (as it relates to student improvement)?
- How will I/we recognise and address what are reasonable outcomes for the time available?

Applying in unfamiliar, different or alternative contexts
- Which aspects of my knowledge of leading collaboration can I/we adapt or modify to suit my/our context?
- Why have I/we chosen these aspects?
- What key ideas will I/we need to be mindful of as I/we go about implementation?

Before you begin

Schools are complex organisations with multiple and competing demands vying for available resources – including *time* to collaborate. Collaboration is important work in schools and can involve many collaborative interactions with different groups across a week. Although the overarching goal might be the same – to support or improve learning outcomes for our students – the *mental effort* required for different components of this work is being underestimated. In this chapter you are being asked to reflect on the purposes for collaboration being undertaken in your context and recognise that there are costs to the individual and the organisation in maintaining these relationships. Exploring the key ideas in this chapter allows us to acknowledge that collaboration cognitively requires time investments for energy, attention and effort for the outcomes expected.

Provocation

How do the educators in your context describe the use of time given or needed for collaborative interactions with a focus on student improvement?

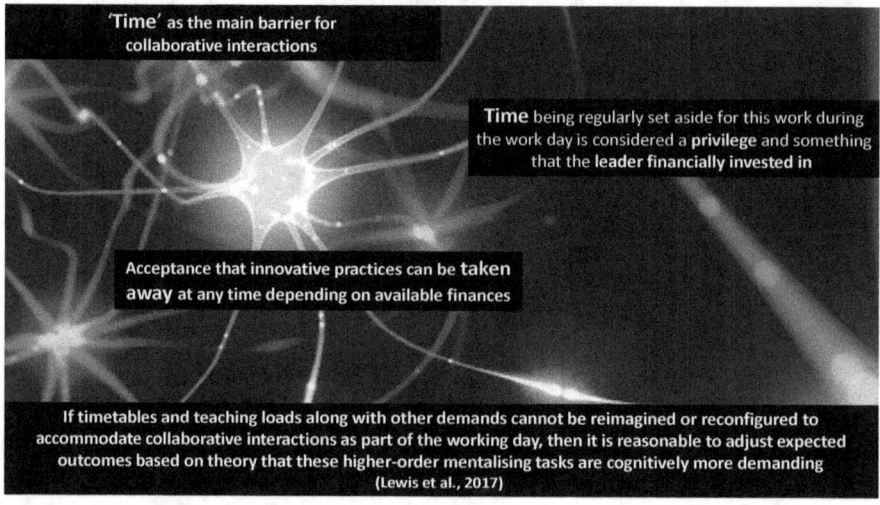

'Time' as the main barrier for collaborative interactions

Time being regularly set aside for this work during the work day is considered a **privilege** and something that the **leader financially invested in**

Acceptance that innovative practices can be **taken away** at any time depending on available finances

If timetables and teaching loads along with other demands cannot be reimagined or reconfigured to accommodate collaborative interactions as part of the working day, then it is reasonable to adjust expected outcomes based on theory that these higher-order mentalising tasks are cognitively more demanding
(Lewis et al., 2017)

Ramona (Head of Department): "It's the ability to invest fully in (the task) when your mind is elsewhere. It is difficult, and much easier on a student-free day where the purpose of that day is allocated to give time [and energy] for that focus area. You can set aside everything else pretty much and you can just work on that project, and you can have more time to actually listen to other people. Even though there's always a set point that you need to get to, it's different. The pace is a little bit different, too. I think time to think through... not be rushed. It is important for the work we are doing."

Questions to ponder

- What are the barriers to collaboration in your context?
- How is collaboration defined in your context? How do you know?

Collaborating with school improvement in mind

Kate (Head of Department): "The collaborations I've been involved in work better when you know a little bit about the person when you have a bit of a connection with them rather than just a group of people who happen to be working together."

The notion of collaboration in schools is an interesting one for me. Type into your favourite browser the word 'collaboration' and look for synonyms. Mine came up with the following:

Similar and opposite words

collaboration

noun

1. cooperation   alliance   partnership   participation   combination   association
   concert   teamwork   joint effort   working together   coopetition

2. fraternizing   fraternization   colluding   collusion   cooperating   cooperation
   consorting   sympathizing   sympathy   conspiring

From Oxford Languages   Feedback

Herein lies a problem: 'collaboration', as described above, occurs in schools on a daily basis in varying ways and for various reasons. However, there has been a shift and separation in what collaboration looks like, sounds like and feels like when it comes to foregrounding it as a strategy for improving student outcomes. While there would be those working in schools who would still use the above descriptions as synonymous for collaboration, others would disagree.

This becomes problematic. Look at the list below to see if any of these resonate for you:

1. Collaboration is any time one or more meet.
2. Collaboration is something we have always done.
3. Collaboration is nothing new.
4. Collaboration can be done on the run.
5. Collaboration – one leads, others follow.
6. Collaboration – sharing the jobs fairly.
7. Collaboration – same time every week.
8. Collaboration – get all tasks done in the time available.
9. Collaboration is too hard to do in our school.
10. Collaboration is not needed as we have the curriculum and assessments provided.

A review undertaken by Vangrieken and associates in 2015 found that different terms were being used to refer to collaboration and were often vaguely defined and often used interchangeably. This is also true of the structures that are put in place to collaborate – for example, *Communities of Practice, Professional Learning Communities, Professional Learning Teams*, to name a few. I *am not* promoting a one-size-fits-all or even common practices. My point here is that there are assumptions that underpin the way we go about collaborating in schools and this has implications for those undertaking and leading the work in the current organisational structures and time available.

> **Sarah (Head of Department):** "It's time, the time in the school day for people to meet. Because everybody is so time poor, you have a set amount of non-contacts for planning... And it's taking a lot more energy and a lot more time to build up momentum."

An important premise is that ongoing school-improvement efforts are best addressed when educators use collaboration as a systematic approach to identify problems of practice and professional dilemmas. These are collectively resolved through shared inquiry, problem-solving and reflection (Donohoo & Velasco, 2016). From a curriculum perspective, collaboration is seen to be beneficial in promoting clarity across and within teams, promoting consistent priorities and creating ownership of the curriculum among those who must teach it. For these reasons, collaboration is viewed as the vehicle, and the benefit is that this strategy supports teachers in taking collective responsibility for the success of each student. In essence, collaboration addresses perceived historical issues of teacher isolationism and practices of individualism. In other words, developing shared beliefs can result in collective action that can positively influence student outcomes. Yet, the implementation and sustainable practices of collaboration, of this type, continue to have varying success in schools.

From a leadership perspective, collaboration moves school improvement to a collective way of thinking, working and being, rather than being left to an individual or groups of individuals. Leaders are learning at the same time as their teachers and use a process of co-construction of thinking that underpins the values and actions of transformational, distributive and instructional leadership. Research has suggested a strong link between professional learning and innovation among leaders who are collaborating with their peers and who are experiencing similar professional dilemmas and problems of practice in leading schools. Leaders who engage with their colleagues in this way model a commitment to an organisational problem-solving approach that has a collaborative discourse focused on learning for ALL at its core. However, although school leaders can value collaboration in theory, in practice it can be viewed as competition to the school's day-to-day operational demands. This is particularly the case when the pace of change seems to be in direct conflict with expected and predetermined targets within designated time frames. Frustration for the strategy (collaboration) can be both a distraction and a cost to collaboration, as educators within schools are being pulled in different directions.

The types of collaboration that lead to innovative practices and improved outcomes for ALL require educators to operate in complex multiple-task environments where they are already particularly prone to disruption from concurrent tasks that compete for their limited attention. As a consequence, resources required to employ collaborative interactions in schools can be seen as competing with other commitments. Determining the best use of the resources available is not as simple or as straightforward as it might appear.

Organisationally, schools reinforce an 'egg carton' or conveyor belt model, which reflects historical values around discipline or subject knowledge being delivered in particular ways – time allocations and resource investments that value certain subjects over others is one example where this is the case. Devaluing one education sector over another is also an example – primary schooling is not as important as secondary schooling and therefore there are different allocations for teacher release. Can you think of other examples?

So, when we think about employing collaboration, we need to unearth those organisational assumptions that leaders and teachers work with. Undertaking this work is important and an effort to identify those possible hidden costs surrounding collaborative interactions with current organisational structures that still operate within historical boundaries.

Acknowledging hidden costs

Much of the literature on collaboration in schools works with an underlying assumption that collaboration is more cost-effective than the effects of silo mentality. That is, the professional isolation and its associated effects cost an organisation more in terms of social capital than the unintended consequences and the challenges associated with collaboration in school settings. Although we might agree that this is not the case, system and school leaders can ignore or not recognise hidden costs when education policies promote, if not mandate, collaboration at all levels of the organisation.

More specifically, mandating collaboration at a system or school level creates challenges when there is more concern with compliance rather than authentic implementation. Even when leaders understand that knowledge, strategy, time, energy and financial resources are required to implement collaboration within an organisation, not all forms of collaboration are equally strong, advantageous or have the desired effect. Leveraging the benefits of collaboration means acknowledging the hidden costs for your organisation so that decisions explicitly address the need to balance collaborative interactions with organisational structures that take account of multiple demands of an educator's work today, not five to 10 (or longer) years ago.

Organisationally, when supports for collaboration are missing or weak, the result can be disorganisation, unclear direction, limited time, haphazard processes and a sense of fragmentation. The complexities within a school make this even more challenging. For example, most organisations would not be required to locate multiple or creative ways to release employees from their day-to-day work requirements for them to meet to collaborate. These same organisations would not necessarily need to reallocate funds to do this either. However, for collaboration to occur in a school context, teachers need to be released, replaced and engage in double the workload – that of providing work for the classroom teacher taking their class and then the work of the collaboration itself. These costs contribute to a school leader's decision to organise collaborative tasks at the conclusion of a workday.

Leaders are well aware that simply organising people into groups is insufficient for establishing effective collaboration. Thoughtful consideration around the structures and procedures for collaboration takes time and involves ongoing review and a willingness to adjust historically embedded school structures that inhibit school-wide collaboration. Teachers know that changing the structures won't necessarily work either when leaders change, too. Investment can be lost if there is not alignment between a new leader's knowledge, values and experience in leading collaboration and the forms of it that already exist.

The investment in cross-discipline or year-level collaboration can be high in ways that go unnoticed. Irrespective of the skills, groups work in different ways because of the dynamics of the individuals. When these groups change, even in small ways, there is a further need to refine communication practices, appreciate others' values systems, negotiate terms and invest in time-consuming meetings. The assumption that *we are all on the same page* because *this is how we do collaboration around here* negates perceptions that reflect individual or team beliefs that cross-discipline or year-level collaboration is unnecessary.

Deeply held beliefs about the *natural order* for some school contexts can see collaboration only necessary within year levels and subject areas. Competing and multiple demands on time can result in collaboration of any type leading to reduced motivation and a loss of productivity if group members unequally contribute and feel that efforts are not worth the result. In addition to this, research has found that group members can also provide unrelated or inaccurate information. The inaccuracies produced by one member of a group can be encoded by other group members to be used on subsequent activities. Research has found that collaboration can also encourage members to forget information that they previously knew, simply because what they knew was never explicitly mentioned during the discussion.

The tensions inherent in effective collaboration are further complicated in education given the apparent contradiction that schools are expected both to compete in the education marketplace and to collaborate. While not mutually exclusive, competition becomes both a distraction and a cost to collaboration. This is because school leaders are being pulled in what can appear to be different directions. While the *Australian Professional Standard for Principals* (2014a) states that Principals are expected to collaborate effectively with other schools and agencies to promote an excellent education system in which all young people can thrive, schools are still measured individually by the success of their school and consequently against other schools. These mixed messages can draw attention away from the increased complexity that collaboration requires. If the supply of attention is limited within an individual and within an organisation, and that attention often flows downstream from a leader's actions (Davenport, 2001), implications for collaboration within and beyond a school must be considered in light of this. In addition, school leaders must contemplate how they will address collaboration within the context of their school, as recent research supports school size contributing to hidden costs associated with implementing collaboration.

Bigger is not always better

In 2002, Leonard's research illustrated that enrolment size of the school influenced the prevailing depth of collaboration and, at that time, collaboration was more common in primary schools as compared with secondary schools. More interestingly, collaboration was not common for teachers in the large and the smallest schools, including combinations of prep/foundation to Year 12, high school/junior high school and middle schools. These findings were further supported more recently (2019), where the authors suggested that in Australia the issue of school size creates tension for scaling up initiatives and affects the number and types of interactions on and between all members of the school community.

The larger a school gets, the more leaders create additional structures to address complexity. On the surface, this might mitigate the issues that surround the issue of size. For example, additional departments or positional roles are created in efforts to reduce the number of people an individual might be responsible for. However, in reality this might mean collaborating with more individuals rather than fewer. When considering collaboration, the larger the school, the more an individual frequently interacts, in many different contexts, with many different individuals, and often repeatedly with many of the same individuals over time.

Dianne (Classroom Teacher): "The size of my school impacts the number of interactions I have. Within the Year 9 team, [and] if I look just at teachers who are teaching English, Maths, Science and Humanities – who I have to deal with and who I may have to email to forward meetings, minutes – that's a group of about 20 to 21 teachers that I have to be in contact with. In addition to that, there's all the other groups that you might be involved with – the other curriculum coordinators, deputies and at least six Heads of Department… So, it is a massive structure. And that doesn't include the kids who are the ones who I would [and should] have the most contact with…"

The more relationships an individual has, the more relationships they need to maintain. A key component of successful collaboration, for school improvement, requires recognition that there is a mutual, reciprocal relationship that is based on trust and an understanding of others' mental states. This is cognitively demanding, as each different type of relationship requires different investments in time. If you think about this in the context of a school, time is precious and often being balanced across many tasks simultaneously. This places limitations on an individual's ability to interact meaningfully. This is not to say interactions in schools are not meaningful. I would argue that this is a large part of the issue for burnout or exhaustion in schools. Educators are trying to maintain large numbers of relationships without the necessary supports in place. Again, I am not saying that support does not exist, I am questioning if the supports that are available are the ones that are right for these new ways of working.

Collaboration is a cognitively complex task

Size matters. The size of a school influences the number and frequency of interactions for individuals, which then has an impact on how and when individuals choose to distribute their social capital in the time they have available to them. Over past years, the expectations for the quality and intentionality of collaborative interactions across and within schools have increased. This is not a bad thing, but the mentalising that takes place for these interactions has been ignored or has gone unrecognised. If we remember that each social bond demands different cognitive requisites and time investment – particularly in face-to-face interactions – then the more relationships, the more socially complex collaboration becomes. Going back to research that suggests we have a limit of about five belief states – that is, we may have beliefs about four other people's beliefs simultaneously at any one time, then higher-order capacities play a crucial role in an individual's ability to manage conversations. Why? Because it involves understanding another person's mindstate and intentions (Dunbar, 2018a). If we think about the types of collaboration that are being employed in schools for student improvement, then we see that it is underpinned by an individual's multiple values and beliefs about learning and the learner. The cognitive demands of this type of sociality required for collaboration in schools is being underestimated!

The number and timing of collaborative interactions (after school, beginning of a term) act as additional pressures on the mental energy levels of individuals. The expectations for the number and differentiated relationships leave those working within these contexts emotionally drained, but with minimal time to rebound before moving on to the next equally important job requirement. Despite Dunbar's research that suggests a decreasing emotional investment is available to distribute among an increasing personal network, current organisational models for schools do not account for this. More importantly, the industrial model of organising teacher work undermines the cognitive energy required to fulfil the interrelated components of the professional standards for teachers and leaders.

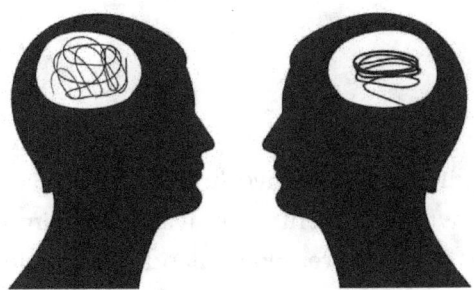

Barriers to collaboration – time, timing and timely

Increased numbers of interactions mean less time available to invest in them. Less time available means less time to maintain *each type* of social bond required for different teams or individuals. Chapter 4 details how these time investments contribute to organisational *cultures of trust*. But for now, apart from the number of people that teachers are expected to interact with, collaboration also requires finding time in the day – somewhere between teaching, planning tomorrow's lessons, marking yesterday's student papers to provide descriptive formative feedback, contacting parents or carers, making sure there is a record of contact for those discussions and possibly attending professional learning that aligns with their personal professional learning expectations. In a recent study where respondents were asked to rank the barriers to collaboration, Time was placed as the number one barrier.

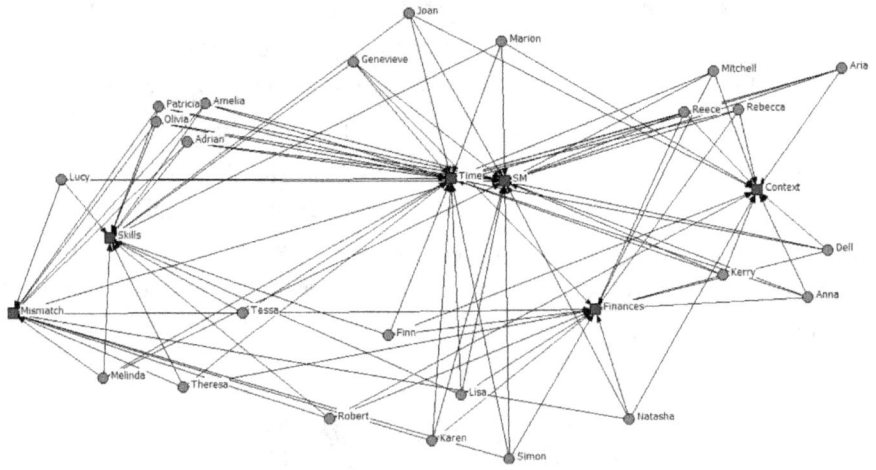

Barriers to collaboration network

Time as a barrier to collaboration supports the notion that collaborative interactions require different investments in time to maintain these relationships. However, current time availability limits the investment possible and thus places increased demands on individuals as they try to manage these relationships to undertake their day-to-day work.

> **Dianne (Classroom Teacher):** "Because of what we've had to fit into the meeting schedule, there hasn't been time to value that other kind of collaboration, such as within a year level, because there are so many other things that we're required to do as part of being part of the school, with the different meeting groups and

working with different faculties. I would say that time is a real issue for collaborating within the busyness of the school."

A school's size can amplify competing demands, but it is important to recognise that the work itself in schools competes for attention on a day-to-day basis. Time to collaborate, within an organisation's structures alongside operational limitations, is given as a main reason for 'collaboration on the run' becoming more and more frequent. Energy for this type of collaboration is being diverted from available energy stores that might otherwise be used to engage in more *productive* collaborative work.

Angela (Classroom Teacher): "Our [Year] 7 meetings are often sabotaged or taken over by other whole-school issues. Even when we do have a Year 7 meeting, about two or three times a term… we don't get much done… it's rushed… we then have to find time to do this work in addition to whatever else has been pushed aside."

Collaboration on the run is defined as those interactions that take place as individuals move from one task or operational demand to another and intended to address student improvement. *Collaboration on the run* supports theory that suggests that our capacity to maintain relationships is limited, when the cognitive demands of sociality require that different types of relationships require different investments in time. The important message here is that the time we have available does not change, but the quality of the outcomes for the types of collaboration does. The strength of these collaborative relationships is also shaped and misshaped by the time available. The strength of these relationships (also known as ties in social network theory) determines the effort, attention and energy that an individual can distribute across them. Without the necessary supports to replenish these stores, individuals can reach saturation points quickly.

Effort, energy and attention – relationships are costly to maintain!

Collaborative interactions require investments that have not been previously recognised or quantified. The overall size of an individual's network has been connected to their cognitive capacity and limited time capacity to maintain these links (Dunbar, 2018a; Tamarit et al., 2018). It has been suggested that 60% of our social effort is divided between just 15 people and connected to the frequency of contact combined with the reciprocal nature of the relationship (Dunbar, 2018a). Data taken from the study from which this book emerged shows the average number of interactions for individuals, their purpose for collaborative interactions, strength of the relationships attributed to these interactions and the frequency with which they interact, have individuals distributing 60% of social effort among *more* than 15 people. In a school context, this is important considering the collaborative interactions intended to deliver improved student outcomes.

Application of a mathematical model proposed by Tamarit et al. (2018) to educators in secondary contexts demonstrated that they are trying to maintain large numbers of relationships. These self-reported relationships were described as strong. In other words, educators in these secondary schools were spreading their social capital 'thickly' among many individuals, which directly contrasts to those findings by Tamarit et al. The findings for the study undertaken in school contexts supports the claim that there is an underestimation of the 'cost' of these collaborative interactions for individuals undertaking this important work.

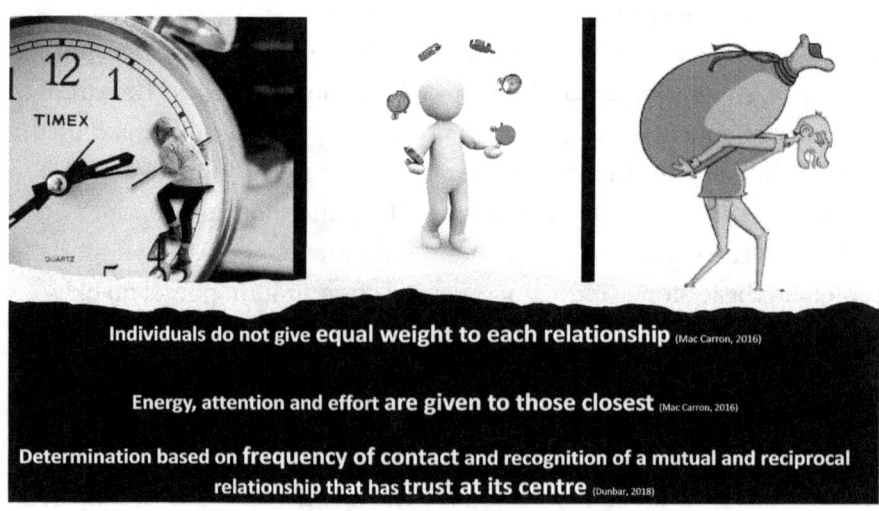

Individuals do not give **equal weight to each relationship** (Mac Carron, 2016)

Energy, attention and effort **are given to those closest** (Mac Carron, 2016)

Determination based on **frequency of contact** and recognition of a mutual and reciprocal relationship that has **trust at its centre** (Dunbar, 2018)

Apprenticing – important but *not* sufficient

Leading schools requires additional and different types of knowledge, training and professional experience. The changing and evolving nature of the work in schools cannot and should not be dismissed. The need for additional and different types of knowledge, training and professional experience to lead collaborative interactions for improved student outcomes is essential. More specifically, investing in 'people skills' remains an integral component to a leader's skill set. Professional learning that is focused on valuing and capitalising the positive power of differences (Kise, 2014) is important, but not sufficient. Developing an understanding of self and others as a tool to support collaboration needs to explicitly address the cognitive demands of sociality and the ways in which this impacts the collaborative interactions being undertaken in different school contexts (for example, primary, secondary, F/P-12 contexts, school size, organisation structures).

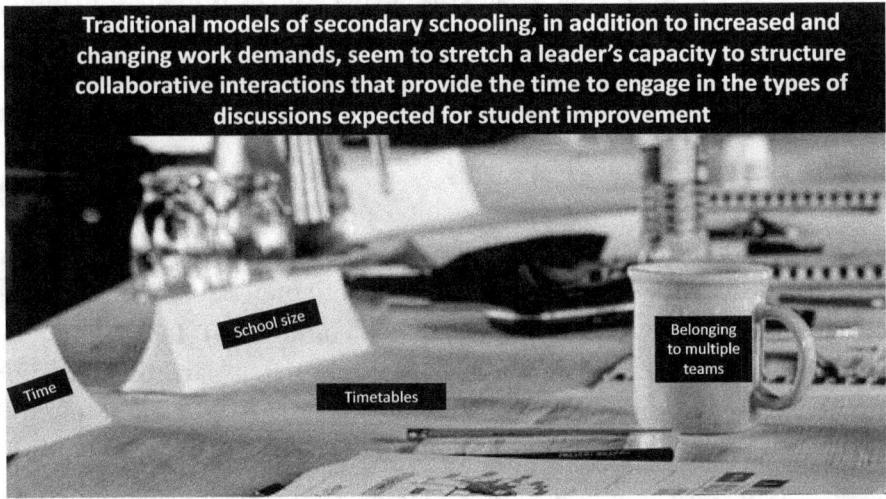

Traditional models of secondary schooling, in addition to increased and changing work demands, seem to stretch a leader's capacity to structure collaborative interactions that provide the time to engage in the types of discussions expected for student improvement

Professional learning that strengthens a leader's understanding in this area can support them further in their decision-making when designing and structuring collaboration as a strategy for improvement. Trust for one another is central to how and why individuals will invest different amounts of time in these different relationships. Yet, as the numbers of students and teachers increase in a school, individuals are having to distribute their social capital across more people, but with more limits on the time available to do so. As a consequence, the expectations for these collaborative interactions need to be adjusted to align with less time to invest in them or look for alternative staffing models that provide more time within the workday.

Conclusion

Collaboration is highly valued as a strategy in school contexts, yet the use of collaboration requires school leaders to apply and work through complications that can emerge from an underestimation of the number of interactions that educators undertake in a typical week combined with the complexity associated with sociality. In part, this can be attributed to the collective descriptions that we use. For example, one teacher and one class or one Head of Department and one team. The issue with these descriptions is that the total number of collaborative interactions is not accounted for. In these circumstances, teachers can be working with more than one Head of Department, have several classes and work with a team of teachers – in effect, interacting with more than a hundred individuals throughout a week. Additionally, maintaining these different relationships requires different investments in time.

Affording time to maintain relationships in schools can be problematic. Day-to-day work demands combined with expectations to collaborate can result in siloed organisational departmental structures viewing whole-school improvement agendas as competition for resources. While collaboration is promoted as a strategy that can mitigate silo mentality, social brain theory contends that there is a limit to the number of relationships that an individual can maintain. If unrecognised or ignored, these complications become barriers for coordinating collaborative efforts to address student outcomes that maximise learning growth for all students. While quantifying the number of relationships, their collaborative purpose, frequency and strength may be relatively simple; quantifying the cost to the individual or the organisation is not as straightforward.

Whichever way one looks at it, relationships cost. Further, relationships vary in substance and form within and between groups, and maintaining each type of social bond demands different cognitive requisites and time investment. Distribution of social effort that generates and maintains a hierarchy of layered sets of relationships within social networks is the result of trade-off between costs and benefits at a given level, and across the different types of demands and resources typical of different levels. Psychologically, these trade-offs are related to the level of trust in a relationship, which is itself a function of the time invested in the relationship (Kolleck et al., 2021; Sutcliffe et al., 2012). This requires attention, which is in increasingly short supply, and yet, it is a critical element for effectively leading and working in schools.

We know that teachers are expected to collaborate with colleagues, students, parents and other professionals to improve student outcomes. It is quite possible the number of people they interact with exceeds 150 – a number quoted in the literature as the typical number of relationships that any one individual can maintain. This is particularly relevant when considering the school context. School size and organisational structures influence the number and type of collaborative interactions. School leaders are being asked to create structures for collaboration. Therefore, how leaders design and structure collaboration within their schools is imperative if they are to protect colleagues from information overload and consequently making it more difficult to implement a strategy designed for school improvement.

Mapping next steps

Underestimating the heavy workload on educators contributes to questions pertaining to long-term sustainability. Recognising *hidden costs* associated with the cognitive demands of sociality can provide leaders with alternative ways of thinking about how collaboration can be more effective in their own contexts. Mapping values and beliefs supports individuals as they collaborate with others to improve student outcomes. Here are some things to try:

1. Create a visual representation of your values and beliefs about learning and learners. What might this look like for others in your teams? Discussion helps take the guess work out of some collaborative interactions for student improvement.

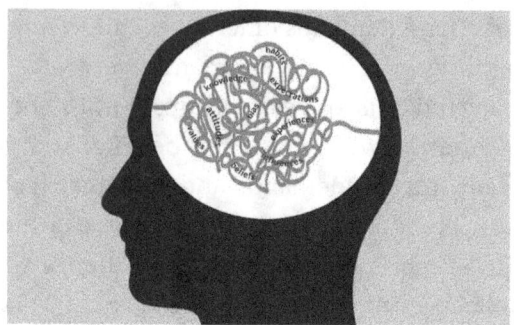

2. Audit the number and types of 'meetings' being undertaken and the collaboration taking place. Seek multiple perspectives to define the purpose for each, the time it takes to get the work done. Do tasks get completed or are they left for others to complete outside of the allocated time?
3. Check in with your teams to see if they engage in '*collaboration* on the run'.
4. Begin to reflect on what outcomes are reasonable in the time available.

Hidden costs can be difficult to recognise when there is a view that "this is just the way it is" or "you can't change schools". Understanding organisational theory can support educators in understanding the distinct features of schools as compared with other types of organisations. In Chapter 4 you will be able to explore the contributions of organisational theory for a leader's preparation to lead collaborative interactions that are socially and cognitively complex. Specifically, collaborative interactions in schools are characterised by differentiated relationships that are reliant on cultures of reciprocal trust that needs to be nurtured intentionally.

Chapter 4
Organisational cultures and differentiated relationships

New to me
- Can I/we explain the importance of understanding organisational theory as it relates to schools?
- What is the relationship between reciprocal trust and time, effort and energy invested in differentiated relationships?
- What additional and different types of knowledge, training and professional experience is required to lead organisational cultures of trust?

Revisiting, reviewing and revising familiar ideas
- Which aspects of organisational theory have been transplanted to our school context? Why is this problematic for our context?
- What do I/we need to explore further to develop cultures of trust in our context?
- What are we willing to remove to accommodate the necessary time required for collaborative interactions that have student improvement at their core?

Applying in unfamiliar, different or alternative contexts
- Which aspects of my knowledge in designing organisational cultures of trust can I/we adapt or modify to suit my/our context?
- Why have I/we chosen these aspects?
- What key ideas will I/we need to be mindful of as I/we go about implementation?

Before you begin

It comes as no surprise that schools are organisations with features that define them in ways that are unlike other organisations. Yet, there still appears to be a persistent approach to treat them just like any other organisation. A fundamental understanding of organisations and the ways in which they work are not usually part of an initial teacher program. Certainly, how schools work is shared and differences in schools possibly explored, but these have a specific focus in preparing beginning teachers, not potential school leaders. The aspects that define schools as different to other organisations is not only important, but contributes to constraints for implementing initiatives. This chapter asks you to contemplate the initiatives in progress in your context and the *organisational theories* that underpin them.

Provocation

Look at the image below and describe how this *is* like working in schools.

Now describe how it is *not* like working in schools.

Questions to ponder

- How do school leaders organise structures for collaboration as a strategy for improvement?
- When might silo mentality NOT be a barrier to collaboration?

Experience and research suggest that many schools that begin various reform efforts **never fully implement** them, and **secondary schools** have less success than **primary schools**
(Askell-Williams & Koh, 2020; Casey, Simon & Graham, 2021; Stringfield, Reynolds & Schaffer, 2016)

Organisationally speaking

When you contemplate schools as organisations, the following might come to mind: learning organisations, social organisations, business organisations, independent organisations, school types, workplaces and organisations within larger organisations. Metaphors abound – gardens, factories, conveyor belts, bridge, gateway, and you can probably add several more. Irrespective of the descriptions, analogies and metaphors about schools as organisations, most of this knowledge and experience is accumulated implicitly or intuitively on the job or indirectly through narratives or previous organisational experiences.

Organisation theory is not a focus for undergraduate or post-graduate teaching degrees. Why would it be? This is not to say that education courses don't discuss the history of schooling and the way schools are organised, but it is reasonable to suggest that inadequate types of knowledge, training and professional experience of organisational theory, as it can be applied in school contexts, places constraints on leadership capacity. For example, organisational structures, processes and decision-making procedures that may have served a school well, when it was smaller or new, can create unintended consequences as the school grows. If a school leader knows that this is not working but is locked into particular ways of thinking because this is how schools operate, then challenging these assumptions from an organisational theory perspective can be lost. However, overlaying organisational theory with schools as organisations is not what I am suggesting here, but rather using organisational theory to place educators in a position to think more consciously about their work in an organisational context with a more nuanced understanding.

Unfortunately, there are many examples where strategies have been lifted from organisation theory and dumped into school contexts without realistic understandings of the differences in these organisations compared to the business world. Collaboration is an example where a powerful practice and strategy can be derailed because the necessary organisational culture and structures have not been addressed to meet the context.

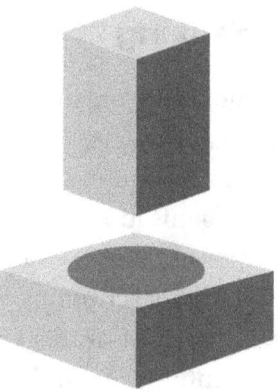

Collaboration, as a strategy for student improvement, is directly impacted by a school leader's ability to create and design environments that enable productive collaborative interactions to occur. These environments are often cognitively complex and require strategic processing capabilities.

Although there have been discussions that describe secondary school organisational structures as moving away from discipline-based or sector-based organisational configurations, many schools still identify their organisational structures as subject-based and or sector-based (Stringfield, et al., 2016). Thus, collaboration is organised based on subjects and year level teams. Organising collaborative interactions in this way proves challenging and problematic for those individuals who work across departments and different year levels. This is because it involves multiple teams to work across and limited time to meet and undertake the expected work.

Structuring collaborative interactions to support student improvement affirms theory around increases in intensity of teachers' work (Beck, 2017). It is also argued here that this also extends to the increased intensity of the work of school leaders. As with teachers, leaders also make rapid professional decisions, are pulled in multiple directions and are required to be innovative problem-solvers. As one leader describes: *"The thing is, there are no answers or no solutions coming from our department about this, so they ask us to do it. But they don't necessarily give us the tools to do that with."* Structuring collaboration as a strategy for improvement, appears a process of trial and error that is based on leader knowledge, experience and skills combined with the complexity of their context.

Australian Professional Standard for Principals (Australian Institute for Teaching and School Leadership, 2014a) expects school leaders to strategically operationalise collaborative practices that will support student improvement. Yet it can be argued that the time needed to explore, learn and apply this knowledge is not being afforded these leaders in the current education climate. Questions arise for policy and practice in this area, particularly when collaboration is viewed as a strategic lever for school improvement.

It is important to recognise that tensions exist between historical hierarchical structures of schools and calls for 'flatter', more distributed leadership structures today. Despite moves to enact fewer hierarchical models with more decentralised decision-making, internal dilemmas create organisational upheaval. On the one hand, we have bureaucratic management practices to deliver consistency and yet on the other hand, expectations and practices of the profession that intend to reflect the complex role of teaching. This can lead to organisational goals and the motives and interests of individual members being juxtaposed. School systems, unintentionally, promote a seesawing back and forth with perceived needs for both centralised *and* decentralised decision-making processes. School leaders wade through this confusion with little support in balancing the school as both a social *and* a bureaucratic system (Askell-Williams & Koh, 2020). The impact this has on the culture of a school can be described as discombobulating, and although accepted as the norm for the way in which schools operate, only adds to the effort, attention and energy in developing collegiality and collaboration among educators working in these school contexts. These organisation contradictions play havoc on the individual investing in the reciprocal trust that is necessary for collaboration.

Reciprocal trust

At an organisational and interpersonal level, trust is an interesting construct for those working in schools. It is directly dependent on the specifics of the roles that exist, an individual's expectations for those roles and perceptions about the relationships that are attributed to them. Now, you may have noticed that throughout the chapters there has been an emphasis on descriptions about the 'individual' and this might seem to be a contradiction to the work of collaboration. The point that needs to be emphasised here is that student improvement requires collaborative interactions that de-privatise the practices of individuals and teams within and across schools (Flanagan et al., 2016). This involves high levels of relational trust and requires school leaders to build and sustain safe environments (Sharratt, 2019) for these individuals to display both high competence and vulnerability (Lipton & Wellman, 2012; Sharratt & Planche, 2016). Unfortunately, this is largely dependent on how an individual ranks the relationship in its importance to invest their effort, limited attention and energy.

At different times of a school year, this can change because it is directly influenced by the purpose of the interactions combined with an individual's own sense of obligation with how often they meet. There is a tendency for stronger emotional connectedness when there is more frequency to the interactions. Relationship decay occurs quickly when opportunities to come together socially and professionally are limited. This can be due to geographical distances and physical challenges of how a school is designed. Decreasing interactions adds to siloing of departments or functions. The benefits of 'knowing' colleagues when faced with challenges or conflict – particularly when individuals were in different departments or year levels – is a sign of reciprocal trust. If individuals are more willing to give 'the other' the benefit of the doubt and/or defend their actions to others, there is more likelihood that the team will do the same.

This supports theory that suggests that *maintaining collaborative interactions* in school contexts is dependent on *cultures of trust* that *require different investments in time*. Unfortunately, schools are not currently designed or funded in ways that leverage these different time investments that are so important to collaborative interactions focused on student improvement. However, all is not lost! School leaders can work with this knowledge to redefine what can be viewed as worthwhile investments when planning for collaborative interactions and expected outcomes in the *time available* (yes, this phrase will become a reoccurring theme throughout this book). What can be ignored in the pace and urgency for outcomes is the necessary trust that is imperative for this important work and can be eroded without intention or realisation. Rebuilding trust within an organisation is a long and arduous process. Actively addressing relationship building is a cornerstone for the successful work of collaboration in schools and can be downplayed because of assumptions around the work and the people leading and doing the work.

Differentiated relationships are socially complex

Individuals can be working with multiple individuals with multiple roles. At the same time, these individuals can be solely responsible for multiple classes and multiple subjects. Working in this way requires an individual to switch and adjust their cognitive efforts to meet the needs of these different types of interactions. In a school context, this can mean a switch from students to teaching team to Head of Department to parents, and in very short time frames and in multiple modes. For this reason, these relationships are described as differentiated and socially complex (Bergman & Beehner, 2015). Maintaining these differentiated relationships requires different investments in time and involves higher-order intentionality, thus described as cognitively demanding.

Up until now, the number of differentiated relationships that educators are expected to maintain to undertake their day-to-day work is being underestimated! The mental energy to switch (sometimes minute to minute) cognitive gears, without time to regroup, leaves educators without the necessary reserves to invest fully in the next equally important series of tasks that make up their day-to-day work. It is the reason that it is more likely that individuals will 'stay close' to where their department or function is located. Largely, this appears to be based on practicalities of their work – movement across and within the school is directly related to the purpose of tasks and collaborative interactions. *Collaboration on the run* becomes an outcome for attempts to maintain the number of differentiated relationships in the limited time available.

Revisiting *collaboration on the run*

Collaboration on the run contributes to silo mentality as individuals focus on what needs to be undertaken in their teams to get the work done efficiently and effectively. While I might disagree with the following sentiments expressed by some educators, it is worth mentioning because it can be operating in school contexts more than imagined. Without recognition or acknowledgement, leaders are less inclined to address it as an issue for whole-school improvement. Where collaborative interactions focus on student improvement within the subject or discipline of participants' departments or year levels – not across departments or year levels – then working across departments and year levels can be viewed as unnecessary.

Collaboration across teams is viewed as nice but not imperative for the work these individuals *need to achieve in the time they have available*. From a social brain perspective, maintaining group cohesion means individuals must be able to meet their own requirements, as well as coordinate their behaviour with other individuals in the group. Leaders who ignore this key element for group cohesion place additional, if not unnecessary, constraints on collaborative interactions. Furthermore, a willingness to coordinate behaviour for collaborative interactions relies on trust being developed through the *frequency* and *strength* of relationships with the time allocated. If leaders expect *high competence and vulnerability* within these collaborative interactions, then how might they apply what they know to support the social complexity in different collaborative interactions? That is, structuring collaborative interactions requires intentionality that reflects understanding of the social complexity required for discussions that focus on student improvement.

Developing organisational cultures of trust with intentionality

Waiting, hoping or leaving schools to become organisational cultures of trust seems an outrageous proposition and highly unlikely for those leading schools. Yet, being deliberate and acting with intentionality can prove problematic without a clear understanding of the time, effort and energy required of socially and cognitively complex collaborative interactions. Leaders may have a very strong and well-articulated vision, but ensuring that their everyday actions align means proactively addressing the number and timing of collaborative interactions with higher-order intentionality effects on behaviour.

As Dianne (Classroom Teacher) says: "You have to switch your brain from interacting with these students in front of you to then deliberating over an email for a parent or your Head of Department, while you are heading off to the next meeting. Then you quickly switch again for the meeting to discuss strategies or assessment tasks with your teaching team."

Each 'switch' requires the individual to forecast the next interaction. That is, predicting what the other might be thinking in response to what will be said and then when it is said, the interpretation of that – a recursive sense making of another's thinking. Organisational trust is shaky when the available time equals distribution of energy, attention and effort among high numbers of collaborative interactions without time to regroup or recover before the next item of business.

Underestimating the number of collaborative interactions across a typical week, their purpose, frequency and strength of these relationships, provides additional reasons for the desire to create stability in what is already perceived as a frenzied environment. As previously stated, cultures of trust are necessary for collaborative interactions and dependent on the time available to invest in them. Therefore, it is reasonable to assume there are associations among cognitive demands of sociality and a sense of trust developed as a consequence of the available time invested in different types of relationships. Therefore, silo mentality is strengthened by the investment of time that individuals inherently give when operating face-to-face with others in their own departments, year levels or business functions.

With limited time available and multiple demands on that time, individuals prioritise those closest to them and in this case, other individuals located in the same space. Educators value collaboration in school contexts, but 'time' is the number one barrier to it. Leaders looking to problem-solve issues that surround competing tensions for silo mentality and collaboration need to explore the associations that exist among organisational structures that promote silo mentality, cognitive limitations with the number of interactions one can have and collaboration, as a strategy for improvement, in their own context.

Collaboration requires knowledge *and* experience with expertise in content, process, product and environment

> **Dianne (Classroom Teacher):** "In Year 9, we have five teachers who are teaching in the senior school, but come back and teach English or Maths or Science in the Year 9 team... Understanding that this makes it more complex... to actually understand the impact... I don't think that they (leaders) really get the complexity of what this looks like for some people's workload, particularly within what they are expected to do."

Collaboration is supported through *purposeful* interactions that require knowledge *and* experience with expertise in content, process, product and environment. Identifying the *value* of collaborative interactions can highlight how and what we conceive as collaboration. The *Australian Professional Standard for Principals and the Leadership Profiles* share expectations for collaboration (see p57), but the interpretation of this varies for individuals because they come to know 'collaboration' contextually.

For some educators, that can mean this knowledge is based on a career in the same school system, same school sector, same department or discipline, same year level... Investing time in unpacking assumptions about collaboration and its various forms can support educators in foregrounding the value of different forms of collaboration. Although research supports the notion that not all forms of collaboration are uniformly robust, beneficial or have the anticipated effect, it is important that leaders place this within context. Dismissing some forms of collaboration based on policy, articles or opinions can actually promote a sense of fragmentation within the organisation. Compliance devalues possibilities for innovative practices. Leaders who ignore the need for teachers to invest time in *their* professional social networks run the risk of these networks being weaker.

The key message here is that swallowing up every minute of every day is underpinned by certain assumptions – what these are need to be surfaced and sometimes challenged. For example, a full-time teaching load is calculated by current enterprise bargaining agreements. There is an allocation of the maximum face-to-face teaching hours, and remaining hours are spent undertaking duties directly related to the teaching and learning program of an *individual* teacher. Although advice is that time should be allocated in usable blocks, it becomes dependent on the timetabled structures that schools use to manage the teaching and learning. Preparation, planning, assessment and collaboration is shaped and misshaped by the tools available to coordinate the individuals of specific groups. Irrespective of being a primary or secondary teacher, the larger the school, the more difficult this becomes to coordinate. At the same time, there can be an assumption that if you are not 'face-to-face' in some meeting or at your computer, then it is not counted as 'work'. Recalculating time investments – even the smallest – across a teacher's workday should not be so quickly rejected.

Teachers value working within their respective departments and recognise the importance of *casual conversations* that are "often responsible for imparting crucial but quite unexpected items of information" (Dunbar, 2010, p363). However, teachers also recognise that working across disciplines is important for student improvement. Valuing and tapping into the wisdom of others is challenging with expectations for current workloads. School leaders can be 'trapped' within silos of knowledge and experience that shape their responses to these problems of practice. Ultimately, the focus for student improvement necessitates school leaders to recognise and move beyond those silos of knowledge and experience that inhibit or create barriers to high-quality learning, teaching and schooling (Australian Institute for Teaching and School Leadership, 2014a). Yet, they are the ones experiencing undue pressure to problem-solve staffing models that support the time required to leverage the collective knowledge and expertise that can be found across disciplines, year levels or functions.

Additionally, concepts of collaboration are entangled within school contexts. That is, collaboration is viewed as both friend and foe of discipline, year level or function integrity. Collaborative interactions can deepen expertise, knowledge and skills within the subject/year level departments, but it is also seen as fragmenting the work to support students' education more holistically. Imploring school leaders to understand the complexities of these polarities (collaboration and silo mentality) is an invitation to explore problems of practice more deeply – particularly when remnants of an old paradigm can travel into a new paradigm in unsuspecting ways, especially in framing these two paradigms as oppositional and antagonistic with each other.

One illustration of this is where the term 'collaboration' is used interchangeably for any interaction that takes place between or among other colleagues for the purpose of work-related foci. Therefore, depending on the knowledge, skills and professional experience of each leader's expectations, outcomes can vary across the same school. School leaders are extremely resourceful and there are numerous examples of school leaders investing in others and themselves as they deal with practical and operational challenges of these polarities. Nevertheless, there is a need to challenge current leadership preparation and support models as being sufficient in providing leaders with what they require to lead collaboration to suit their diverse organisational complexities.

Apprenticing – important but not sufficient

Leading schools requires additional and different types of knowledge, training and professional experience. Envisaging ways to lead collaboration where silo mentality is not a barrier can be problematic if school leaders have not looked at the organisation with a panoramic view. The familiar can stand in the way of innovation and yet taking what is familiar and reimagining its use has possibilities for bridging silo mentality and working in service of collaboration for school improvement. One way to address the collaboration and silo-mentality polarities is to reverse-engineer leadership roles. Start with purpose and then look for examples in schools beyond your 'silo'. Borrowing from others is what we do in education – the problem is that we don't usually start with purpose.

Efficiency is often the main driver for decision-making and this does not always align with purpose. One leader shared an approach that their school used in solving tensions that arose in their context. After explorations for more than a year, they came to the decision to use cross-curricular priorities or general capabilities as overarching leadership roles. This aligned to purpose – supporting student improvement more holistically than previous approaches. Role descriptions were co-constructed and deliberate in design. Applicants for these roles knew from the outset the purpose and collaborative nature of the work. Most importantly, the leaders, once appointed, were provided with very specific and targeted professional learning. The principal of this school understood the challenge for leaders to move from binary thinking to embracing contradictions and the paradoxical or overlapping perspectives (Donnelly, 2020).

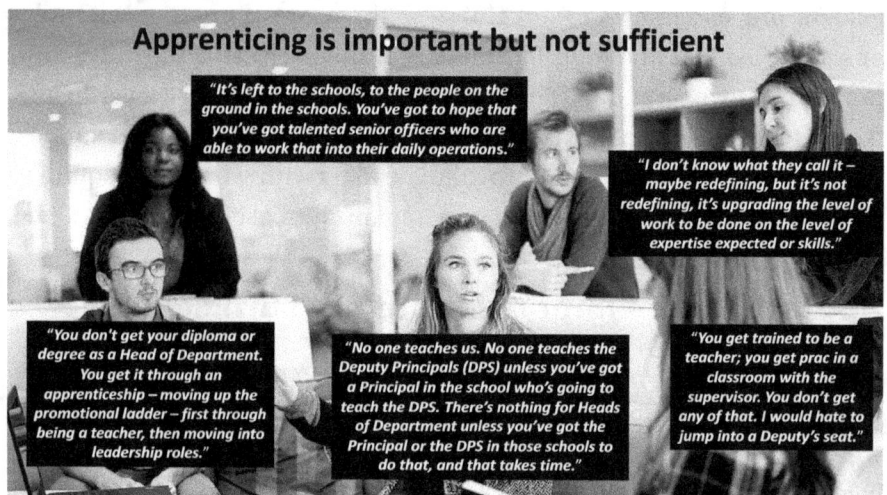

In secondary contexts specifically, you can see evidence in departmental structures that foreground subjects or disciplines, and yet there are expectations to support students holistically. This proves challenging with an either/or mindset. At the same time, leaders work to employ familiar structures (timetables, new leadership roles) to mitigate issues created by the increasing size of their school, and yet appear perplexed, surprised or frustrated when other issues (communication, lack of understanding) became evident as a consequence of these 'new' structures. School leaders require knowledge and skills in working with complexity and systems of 'complication' rather than viewing them as 'enemies of the state'. Complexity in secondary schools is accepted. However, preparation of leaders using an apprenticeship model compounds preconceived ways of working and, in some cases, promotes a reductionist and mechanistic approach that does not account for the intricate relationships among and between the various parts of the organisation as a whole.

Conclusion

As an organisation, schools present leaders with multifaceted and complex macro and micro opportunities and constraints. The social, political, historical, economic and cultural perspectives that a leader works within challenges current preparation pathways that ignore the inclusion of organisation theory with particular reference to schools as organisations. Defining the characteristics of schools – as compared with other types of organisation – assists in issues that arise when transplanting organisation practices to schools without adjusting, accommodating or making use of context. This can be seen in strategies like collaboration where leaders fully support the idea in theory, but the pragmatics for sustainable practices is problematic.

Collaborative interactions in schools are focused on a singular, albeit umbrella, purpose – to improve student outcomes. De-privatising the practices of individuals and teams within and across schools is underpinned by certain assumptions about teaching, learning and the profession. Bringing educators together in efforts to collaborate involves high levels of relational trust and requires school leaders to build and sustain safe environments for these individuals to display increasing expertise and openness. The work of a teacher, including curriculum design and delivery, can mean that individuals are working with multiple individuals with multiple roles. At the same time, teachers can be solely responsible for multiple classes and/or multiple subjects. For this reason, these relationships are described as differentiated and socially complex. Maintaining differentiated relationships requires different investments in time and involves higher-order intentionality. Switching from one type of relationship to another without the time to adjust and reset is cognitively demanding.

Collaboration on the run contributes to silo mentality as individuals focus on what needs to be undertaken in their teams to get the work done efficiently and effectively. From a social brain perspective, maintaining group cohesion means individuals must be able to meet their own requirements, as well as coordinate their behaviour with other individuals in the group. Leaders who ignore this key element for group cohesion place additional, if not unnecessary, constraints on collaborative interactions. The expected outcomes leave those working within these contexts emotionally drained but with minimal time to rebound before moving on to the next, and equally important, job requirement. Developing organisational cultures with intentionality can prove problematic without a clear understanding of the time, effort and energy required of socially and cognitively complex collaborative interactions.

Collaboration requires knowledge *and* experience with expertise in content, process, product and environment. *Leading schools requires additional and different types of knowledge, training and professional experience* that moves beyond the apprenticeship model as being sufficient in preparing leaders with foundational organisation theory. Organisation theoretical concepts when contextualised, rather than transplanted into schools, can support leaders in adopting ideas, but with adaption for the difference and dynamics of schools as organisations.

Mapping next steps

1. In thinking about the power of collaboration and accessing the collective wisdom for improving student outcomes, it is important to identify when and where *collaborative interactions* take place.
2. In the previous chapter, you audited the number and types of *meetings* taking place across the school. You also looked at purpose. Create a visual diagram of these and share it with your school community. Is this a realistic view of what is taking place?
3. How many of your colleagues and peers define what takes place in these *meetings* as collaborative interactions?
4. Identify the *time* set aside for these *meetings* and the actual time invested. What do you notice? What do others notice?
5. What are the expected outcomes for these collaborations?
6. Are these reasonable in the time available? How do you know?
7. What might you adjust or change? Why?
8. What might others suggest? Why?

Building a picture of the collaborative interactions that take place within a school context supports leaders in recognising organisational behaviours that reflect a naturally occurring phenomena – silo mentality, which occurs in every type of organisation. In schools silo mentality is promoted by school structures, the number of interactions taking place and the frequency of interactions over time. Chapter 5 discusses how silo mentality can act as a self-protection mechanism and although can be viewed as a barrier to collaboration, can also be leveraged for student improvement.

Chapter 5

Silo mentality as a construct of function, knowledge and experience

New to me
- Can I/we explain silo mentality as a construct of function, knowledge and experience?
- Why is silo mentality considered both an organisational dysfunction and a strength?
- What additional and different types of knowledge, training and professional experience is required to recognise and leverage silo mentality within school contexts?

Revisiting, reviewing and revising familiar ideas
- Which aspects of silo mentality exist in your context? Why is this problematic or advantageous for both individuals and the organisation?
- What do I/we need to explore further to leverage silo mentality in our context?
- What is assumed prior knowledge and experience in our context when it comes to leading collaborative interactions for student improvement?

Applying in unfamiliar, different or alternative contexts
- Which aspects of my/our knowledge of silo mentality or leadership apprenticing can I/we adapt or modify to suit my/our context?
- Why have I/we chosen these aspects?
- What key ideas will I/we need to be mindful of as I/we go about implementation?

Before you begin

Have you ever experienced a school where the structures are based on traditional models of subject or discipline and have *universal, ingrained, institutional practices and procedures*? These structures immunise against reform efforts by building a 'collective consciousness' that believes it is *inconceivable to behave in any other way*. I would like a dollar for each time I have been told: *"Sorry, that's just not possible, it's just the way it is!"* This chapter explores how these practices contribute to *silo mentality* and describes it as a *construct of function, knowledge and experience*. Importantly, silo mentality can be both an *organisational strength* and *problematic* to improvement initiatives. Throughout this chapter you are invited to *reflect on how silo mentality can go unrecognised*.

Provocation

Questions to ponder

- How do school leaders recognise silo mentality?
- Where have you witnessed silo mentality in school contexts?
- In what ways does silo mentality prove problematic for educators?

Silo mentality as organisational dysfunction

The first reference to silos as a metaphor in organisational behaviour came from Neebe (1987), where he referenced grain silos as an example of how parts of organisations function in a manner disconnected from the others. Vertical divisions and horizontal functions operate in such a way that departments fail to exchange knowledge or information – either deliberately or unintentionally.

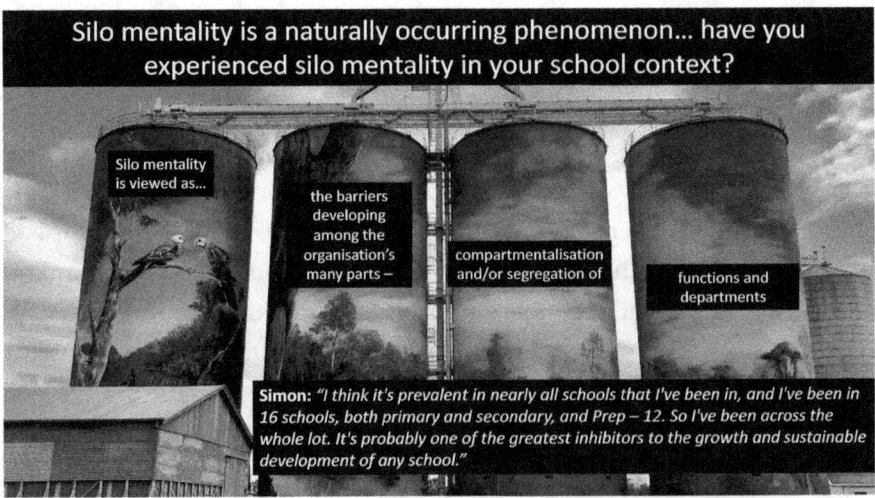

Even though silo mentality is a naturally occurring phenomenon, it proves to be one that leaders from all types of organisations find challenging to address. As its name suggests, silo mentality results in organisational artefacts and practices splintering or fragmenting. From an organisational perspective, the whole is segmented and viewed as a sum of its parts, impacting negatively on the formation of relationships between individuals and within teams. These divisions hinder internal and external collaboration, which impacts organisational learning that prevents the achievement of high organisational performance and sustainability. Therefore, silos – and more specifically silo mentality – are viewed as a form of organisational dysfunction, and various authors (Forsten-Astikainen et al., 2017) would suggest that despite the tools we have available to disseminate information and to ensure development of wide-ranging skills, knowledge mobility and learning, silos continue to exist within all types of organisations today, including schools.

I would suggest that silos have been entrenched in the way we have historically structured schools to reflect a discipline- or age-based approach to develop specific knowledge. For schools, silo mentality can appear to be the natural order of the way we do things around here. It can also be an indication for why collaboration can prove to be challenging in some school contexts. Underlying assumptions about how schools operate can have significant influence in the way silo mentality can emerge as barriers for individuals and teams when collaborating for student improvement.

Collaboration is often seen as the way to mitigate the issues that arise as a consequence of silo mentality. However, this has not been found to be entirely true. Even if the right processes are in place for collaborative behaviour, structural walls can impede the right connections. Geography and organisational design can create physical silos that impede information flow – think about the physical layout of some secondary school contexts or large primary schools. The way they are organised by year levels, subject departments and vocational pathways can be highly collaborative, but also 'balkanised' – effectively segregated from the rest of the school. If whole-school improvement is the objective, then leaders potentially face negative implications for designing, implementing and maintaining whole-school learning and improvement.

> **Sarah (Head of Department):** "We sit in a room doing our thing, collectively. It's a silo and sometimes we might talk to others. We might show and tell what we've done, but we're doing that work, separate to everybody else."

Leaders instinctively address this through restructuring, redesign and revisioning the ways in which collaboration takes place. However, creating new teams, new times and new approaches can eventually lead to new silos rather than mitigating the effects that lead to the issues in the first place. This is not to say that leaders should not explore these options, but what is crucial is that they recognise the signs that silo mentality is becoming a barrier to whole-school improvement goals. Despite silos being viewed as an organisational dysfunction, they also offer a practical way for organisations to operate efficiently and therefore can be considered as an organisational strength. Rather than being dismissed out of hand, silos can offer opportunities and possibilities for achieving whole-school improvement goals, particularly when leaders understand how to leverage and value what they offer an organisation.

Silo mentality as an organisational strength

Silos have their place – or at least this is true for those aspects that promote expertise and that can be leveraged for building capacity rather than isolating groups and subgroups. Despite the negative effects that working within a silo can produce, it can also provide an insular protection that can reduce the distractions and demands from outside the department or function that they represent. This can direct the focus and efficiency of delivering specific goals that pertain to a single organisational department or function. Expertise, depth of knowledge and skills can increase as a result of this focus without interference.

In a school context, departments based on curriculum subjects or age-related year levels are highly valued in supporting the growth of discipline knowledge and expertise within those that work within that space. Year levels and subject departments represent an influential context for teachers developing an organisational identity and sense of collegiality within those organisational spaces. The complexity of people alongside differences that exist within departments or year levels can be a source of creativity and learning that is highly beneficial to an organisation. However, organisational capacity across loosely coupled silos requires coordination and communication (Lloyd, 2016). In other words, collegiality and cooperation does not equal shared understanding. Therefore, in order to coordinate efforts to make the most of the expertise that can reside within these silos, it is necessary to create, maintain and sustain leadership with panoramic and complexity thinking across boundaries to ensure the organisation benefits as a whole. Compartmentalising is a natural way to manage large and complex organisations. However, leaders need to be aware that they, too, operate within a silo and self-reflect on how this might be affecting whole-school improvement efforts.

Silo mentality and collaboration as polarity thinking

Silo mentality and collaboration can be viewed as polarities. Johnson (2012) defines polarities as interdependent pairs that can support each other in pursuit of a common purpose. Yet, they can also undermine each other if seen as an either/or problem to solve. Polarities at their essence are unavoidable, unsolvable, unstoppable and indestructible. In the literature, silos are viewed as a problem and something to be "dismantled, torn down, dealt with" through the implementation of collaboration. Consequently, collaboration and the various forms of collaborative practices – professional learning teams, professional learning communities, communities of practice – are viewed as 'the answer' to dealing with silo mentality. Rather than being regarded as an 'either/or' option, maybe it is possible to conceive an alternative relationship between silo mentality and collaboration. Rather than seeing silos and collaboration as an either/or proposition, map the positive and negative aspects of each and leverage the differences to support the change process (see the end of this chapter). In other words, maximise the advantages and minimise the disadvantages. Identifying the issues, fears or problems of silos and collaboration within your context enables more informed decisions about action steps to reach a common goal. So, before you begin mapping, consider the following...

Silo mentality is promoted by school structures, number of interactions required and frequency of interactions

Breaking down silos – or silo mentality – in organisations appears to be a never-ending pursuit and one that is perceived as often getting in the way of delivering school-improvement efforts (Hargreaves, 2019). Traditionally, the organisational psychology literature views silos as *conscious, rational and objective entities* (Cilliers & Greyvenstein, 2012, p2). Consideration must be given to this being *a product of our cognitive constraints as humans*. The size of your organisation matters. In other words, collaboration as a strategy for school improvement relies on the entire school developing social capital that supports growing student outcomes, and yet it appears that the rate of this occurring might be *somewhat slower than even first thought possible.* Setting targets is important, but not if they are unrealistic in the time available.

The hard evidence on achieving excellence in education points to the need for educators to affirm the fundamental *interdependency of their work* (Kilgore & Reynolds, 2011) and, rather than viewing the parts as separate, realise how they are interrelated and interact to achieve a goal (Senge, 2012). Currently, schools as organisations are highly compartmentalised, with teachers organised into departments by their subject matter specialty or year level. I would argue that, for the most part, collaborative interactions are designed with financial, human and structural constraints in mind rather than purpose. I realise that these claims may be unpopular and for some unfounded, but I would ask you to take the time to step back and contemplate the way collaboration works in your context. If collaborative interactions are structured in ways that reflect constraints rather than purpose, then this can seldom generate the crosscutting ties needed for teachers to *acquire the larger context* in which their work is positioned (Kilgore & Reynolds, 2011).

Cultures of individualism in teaching can often be mistaken for a single person or persons. Yet, departments, teams and year levels can also fall into this category. *Silo mentality is a construct of function, knowledge and experience*, and although recognised by individuals, is often bounded by the *experience* and *role* of that individual. For example, a teacher working in the same school, same year level over time or a leader in the same system, school and role over time will have access to certain knowledge and experience. The same applies to school leaders.

As a *construct of function*, silo mentality is a *consequence of designing structures to manage large numbers of people* as an organisation grows larger. Think about it: 'departments' that look after finance, parents, tuckshop, maintenance, cleaning, sub-schools, curriculum disciplines and you could possibly think of more. When a school is small, many of these jobs are undertaken by a few people, and quite often one person will have multiple roles. If you have ever been to or had experience in a one-teacher school or those schools with a Teaching Principal, you will know what I mean!

As a school gets larger, we bring on others to take on these roles and, over time, we can end up with schools within schools. On the surface, it seems that 'growing' your school is a good thing. One could hold the view that increasing student numbers correlates to school performance. In other words, parents are choosing your school because their perception is that student numbers increasing equates to a stronger-performing school (dependent on definitions).

However, as a school grows, *silos naturally occur* in response to managing the operations of a larger organisation. The larger a school gets, the more layers. Leaders create additional structures to address complexity and, along with it, more leadership roles. Each member of the leadership team is given a portfolio of duties that they manage and are accountable for. We do this to make sure that each person has equitable workloads, strengths utilised and, in some rare cases, side-lining individual inadequacy to minimise impact.

Depending on the *knowledge and experience* of those designing these organisational structures, staffing models will reflect *what is available to decision-makers*. It is the reason that collaboration is so highly valued and necessary in addressing silo mentality. Collaboration is a way to *boundary cross* and build that collective wisdom that can be locked away and not easily accessed when silos or silo mentality are operating intentionally or unintentionally. Analysing the number, frequency and purpose of collaborative interactions within current organisational structures begins a process of leveraging the strengths of silos to develop collective wisdom.

Bringing attention to the underestimated or the unnoticed

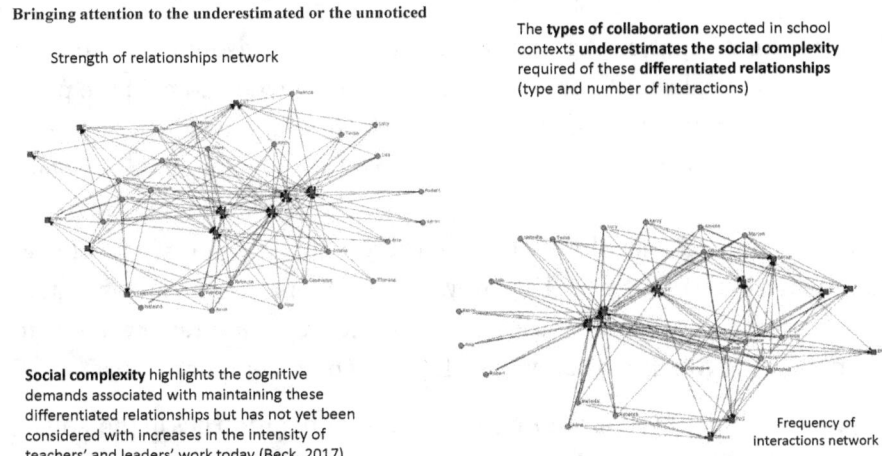

Bringing attention to the underestimated or the unnoticed

Strength of relationships network

The **types of collaboration** expected in school contexts **underestimates the social complexity** required of these **differentiated relationships** (type and number of interactions)

Social complexity highlights the cognitive demands associated with maintaining these differentiated relationships but has not yet been considered with increases in the intensity of teachers' and leaders' work today (Beck, 2017)

Frequency of interactions network

Rethinking organisational structures for collaboration

In 2010, the McKinsey & Company report entitled *How the World's Most Improved School Systems Keep Getting Better* suggested that systems and therefore schools within those systems, moving from *Great to Excellence*, required innovative ways to address the administrative and operational barriers that can get in the way of focusing on pedagogy and leadership. This is particularly pertinent for schools growing rapidly. In other words, leaders who have schools growing at such a rate might not have given time to this as an issue because they are too busy managing the growth of the school and all that goes with that! It can be like the frog in the boiling water analogy... However, this can result in multiple demands on teaching staff, mis- or lack of communication, confusion as to priorities and feelings of being pulled in too many directions. Although it is possible to think that this issue only pertains to increasing school size, or schools of a certain size, I would ask you to review latest staff opinion surveys and media feeds on teacher workload and attrition rates. The work in schools today to improve student outcomes is more sophisticated and underrated in its complexity. The simplicity of solutions put forward reflect a causal mindset that do not account for human factors or day-to-day variables that reflect complex organisations.

Moving from analysis to harnessing collective wisdom for student improvement calls for boundary-crossing leaders who can help the parts work together to strengthen the whole. This is supported by Willcock (2013), who states that organisation 'connectors' can play an important role in relationship management across the organisation. However, I would contend that this is only feasible when we are all willing to rethink basic assumptions about how schools work. As previously stated, restructuring alone is not the answer, and planning and review needs to be integrated with organisation development on an ongoing basis.

In part, the difficulty in promoting cross-silo cooperation lies in the 'softer' aspects of culture, including strong values, a highly egalitarian culture and clear organisation communication (Dean, 2010) and therefore, scholars who analyse human systems, such as Senge (2012), argue that *all members* of an organisation need an understanding of the big picture – the challenges and strengths in other parts of the organisation. Consequently, social brain theory adds value and shines light on possible barriers to school-improvement initiatives that involve strong cultures that can promote silo mentality, yet still look at using collaboration as a whole-school strategy for improvement.

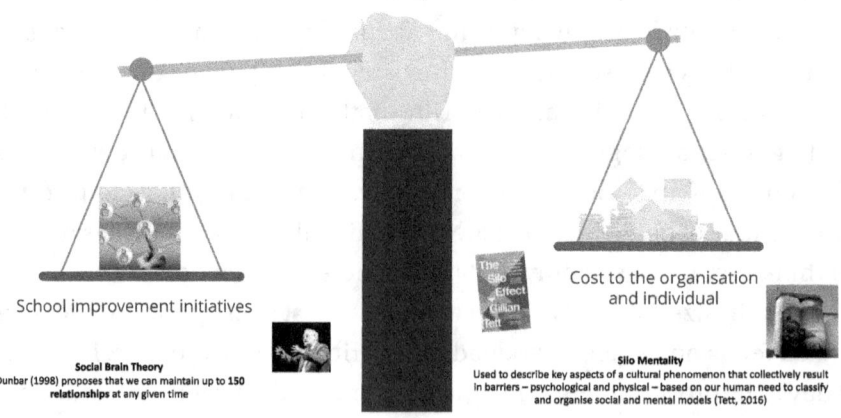

School leaders weigh up decisions

School improvement initiatives

Social Brain Theory
Dunbar (1998) proposes that we can maintain up to 150 **relationships** at any given time

Cost to the organisation and individual

Silo Mentality
Used to describe key aspects of a cultural phenomenon that collectively result in barriers – psychological and physical – based on our human need to classify and organise social and mental models (Tett, 2016)

Assuming prior knowledge and experience is enough to lead, manage and innovate for change

The belief that silos and silo mentality prevent achievement of high performance and organisational sustainability have been long recognised as a tangible problem needing to be addressed (Waal et al., 2019). As one leader suggested, silo mentality is *one of the greatest inhibitors* to the growth and sustainable development of any school. However, silo mentality is usually more recognisable for people that operate or have operated in different roles.

More specifically, individuals can recognise different silos operating within their contexts, for example, leadership teams, teaching teams, junior secondary sector teams, senior secondary sector teams or subject-based teams. In other words, silo mentality is a *construct of experience*, defined by the activities of the roles the individual performs, within the specific context it is performed. For example, a teacher of Science in the junior secondary identifies their role, subject area and sector as defined focus for their energy, attention and primary purpose for interactions. The more experience in different roles and in different school contexts, the more likely one is to recognise silo mentality. Consistent with other research, individuals are able to describe clearly delineated 'cultural tribes' that people identify with, and tightly defined teams that people are motivated to work for and with (Waal et al., 2019, p2). However, silo mentality can go unrecognised by what an individual can and can't see.

In schools, one silo can be enveloped by a larger silo – teaching team, subject discipline, junior or senior secondary school and education sector. Silo mentality, therefore, is bounded by the experiences of leaders and dependent on opportunities to move beyond their own silo. In other words, leaders are more likely to recognise silos in their own organisation or others, but may not necessarily recognise the one that they belong to.

Silos enveloped by larger silos and created in my own image

For example, if school leaders have always worked within the one education system and have minimal experience with other systems, then although they may have worked across schools, silo mentality operating at that level can go unrecognised. One silo is enveloped by a larger silo. Education systems can create siloed knowledge and experience for leaders without realising it.

Leader development programs and professional learning reflect education system priorities that may, or may not, match what school leaders require in their school context. Assumptions about leadership readiness results in a disconnect between assumed knowledge and actual knowledge and highlights an imbalance between experiences arranged by the system and those that leaders have to 'pick up' informally. This assumed prior knowledge and experience can be problematic for leading, managing and innovating for change. At a school level, leaders know this and continually invest financial resources to develop leadership capacity within their schools. They acknowledge that these investments address the complexities that arise with diverse capabilities of their current leadership team. Perceived as 'bespoke', there can be duplication across schools and education systems. At a macro level, it can be concluded that current preparation for leadership is insufficient or ad hoc, with assumed prior knowledge and experience of leaders not enough to lead, manage and innovate for change. From the micro level, some leaders would argue that it almost takes a little bit of detraining, in terms of people operating in a way that they know is in their mind efficient and delivers some results.

Apprenticing is not sufficient to lead schools today

Collective understanding and ways of working can prove problematic in schools for new and existing staff who move into new roles. This is to say that there can be 'hidden' or accepted practices that would not necessarily be addressed in an induction process for new staff and, as the school grows and staff change, the more challenging this becomes. Staff continue to operate in the ways they have come to know concepts and practices. *Silos can be a construct of presumed knowledge.* The apprenticeship model in preparing leaders is necessary but not sufficient. It presumes that those leaders who are mentors have the necessary prior knowledge and experience to lead, manage and innovate for *today's education landscape*. The apprenticeship model relies on the 'luck of the draw' and an assumption that all leaders are created equal.

It also assumes that prior knowledge and experience is enough to lead, manage and innovate for change. This is problematic as knowledge and experience differs greatly among leaders, and this influences the perceived depth of understanding of what teaching and leading look like today as compared to 10 years ago. As previously stated, a leader's knowledge, experience and skill reflect the silo they are enveloped in. Leaders can become stuck in leadership tensions that arise from an 'imagined past reality' with an 'imagined current reality'. In other words, comparing the day-to-day demands of working in schools today is not the same as 10 years ago. Silo mentality can be a function of experience, and for some leaders this means recognising but not necessarily addressing challenges teachers are facing today. At the same time, a full-time teacher load as compared with a Head of Department, Deputy Principal or Principal amplifies competing tensions.

Created in my own image – silos reflect the personality, values and beliefs of the leaders

Silos reflect those leading them. In other words, the silos reflect the personality, values and beliefs of the leaders within it. In effect, silos are 'created in my own image'. This is not difficult to understand when considering the pathway for promotion in schools. Interviews with leaders across three school systems identified that the apprenticeship model as the main avenue for moving into leadership roles. This model is viewed as positive and has worked well in the past, but now educators would challenge that it is sufficient to lead schools today. Different education sectors and tertiary institutions provide various programs and courses. While they provide a short-term boost to skills, knowledge and practices of those individuals that make the choice to attend or participate, these still rely on an apprenticeship model for putting theory into practice.

One consideration could be for schools to invite an *insider-outsider* to observe and provide feedback. A pair of neutral eyes may see what we are blind to! Shifting insular focus can be challenging in the fast-paced school environment. One way to address this issue is by employing *insider-outsider* boundary-crossing mentors to work with and alongside schools to explore silo mentality in their contexts. This partnership can support leadership teams and contribute to conversations that promote more panoramic views of the specific school context. However, the selection of this partner is important and unlike in some education jurisdictions where dedicated school-improvement units offer a range of services, there can be a sense of unease and absence of deliberate relationship building and trust. Recognition of silo mentality needs conditions of high trust and strong relationship building. These are very difficult to create when those working in these environments feel that they are being judged with a focus of being 'caught out'. Therefore, the *skill set*, and *qualities* of the *insider-outsider* are not based on a selection of convenience or a tokenistic offering. There is intentionality around the who and why of the individuals employed in these roles.

The addition of a knowledgeable other (Sharratt, 2019) is specifically selected to provide ongoing support and mentoring for leaders and therefore needs to be *someone outside the system*. Being outside the system brings a *sense of trust* that is paramount. Working with a mentor that is not sitting in 'judgement' or influencing (positively or negatively) promotional opportunities brings opportunities for more openness. Yet, it is essential that this partner has *insider knowledge and understanding of schools as organisations today*. Developing trust within these partnerships begins with the selection of a partner who has credibility based on experience, extensive knowledge and relationship building.

Apprenticing – important but not sufficient

Leading schools requires additional and different types of knowledge, training and professional experience. Collaboration for school improvement necessitates that school leaders have deeper understanding of the relationships between collaboration and silo mentality.

Building panoramic views (boundary crossing) can support leaders in recognising and addressing competing tensions that contribute to silo mentality

Recent research that used integrated findings (quantitative and qualitative data) produced conclusions that reveal the apprenticeship model of the past is important, but not sufficient in preparing school leaders for educational contexts today. Competing commitments and competition for scarce resources is inevitable in large organisations and schools are no exception. Furthermore, schools as complex organisations are defined by the intricate and interconnected relationships of their various parts, but this has not historically been a focus for professional learning for leaders. The natural state for complex organisations is a certain chaos rather than stability, but because of organisational structures like timetables and calendar intervals that fit a conveyor belt model of production, predictability is expected. However, this creates tensions for leaders and teachers who work within these complex organisations. This makes schools less predictable and worthy of more time invested in supporting leaders' knowledge, experience and training for working with these types of organisations.

If a school's culture reflects those who are leading these contexts, then setting aside time to explore and articulate the values and beliefs of those leaders is important work but conditional on the importance that is placed on the processes used to undertake it. Bringing forth values and beliefs does not always mean that these are the ones in action. Alignment is more difficult when silo mentality is evident but not necessarily recognisable to those within it. Questioning what values and beliefs your actions are demonstrating, *and how do you know*, is the first step, but intentionally seeking to uncover misalignment means going beyond surveys. Surveys are important and as data-collection data tools are efficient, but they can leave out or ignore multiple viewpoints, perspectives and standpoints that draw on strengths of both quantitative and qualitative approaches in making sense of our own and others' understanding of their workplace.

- Speak to the people at the 'coal face' with genuine curiosity.
- Listen, listen, listen.
- Be open to criticism – there are often some gems if we recognise them.
- Some people will act as your barometer, they will provide you with perceptions of what is working well and not so well. Embrace this as feedback and early-warning signs.
- Continually reflect on the messages we send to those we work with through our language and interactions. We can't escape that our actions and inaction communicate our intentions to others. We need to continually check and clarify our intent with the messages that are being received.

Through these processes leaders are provided with an assemblage of evidence of various types to build and support the arguments that when taken as a whole necessitates a conclusion that withstands critical scrutiny. Adopting this approach addresses a need to reconcile different philosophical viewpoints and offers specific ideas as to what amounts to knowledge, but does not profess to present a definitive worldview. Underpinning this approach is analysis that will be strengthened beyond what would have been possible with a singular paradigm.

Conclusion

The very *nature of traditional schooling* can promote silos and silo thinking. Silos, within a school environment, are the product of systems to classify, manage and organise the various operational demands. In other words, silos come into existence to organise the functions of the day-to-day running of a school. Silo mentality is promoted by school structures, the number of interactions necessary and the frequency of interactions to undertake day-to-day work demands. Silo mentality has been described in the literature as organisation dysfunction, but they serve as an organisational strength because of the expertise that can be contained within them. When leaders are able to recognise them, they can leverage the best parts of silos to move their school-improvement agendas in the right direction.

If leaders ignore silos or silo mentality, they run the risk of having fragmented change agendas, miscommunication, low morale, stressed and burnt-out teachers and a never-ending course of 'swings and roundabouts'. One contributing factor in school contexts is assuming prior knowledge and experience is enough to lead, manage and innovate for change. Apprenticing is not sufficient to lead schools today. If silos reflect the personality, values and beliefs of the leaders and are known to be created in a leader's own image, then *leading schools requires additional and different types of knowledge, training and professional experience.*

Mapping next steps

To begin the process:

- **Recognise** that this polarity exists and the effects that it has in your context.
- **Identify** the value and purpose of having the best of both (silos practices and collaborative practices) within your context – create a goal statement that reflects this.
- **Map the polarity** by examining the advantages and disadvantages of both (see the example overleaf).

Improved Student Outcomes through Improved Teacher Practices

Silo Practices	Collaborative Practices
Positive	
Specialist knowledge	Shifting from me to we
Contextualised and localised decision-making	Contributing to a common goal
Efficiency	Inquiry and collective problem-solving approach
Competitiveness between departments	Sharing practice, knowledge and problems
Initiatives, resourcing and practices contextualised	Innovation as part of learning
Operations specialised	Efficient
Individual expertise promoted	Rich dialogue
	Common language
	Valuing difference
	Promoting high levels of trust
Negative	
Us and them thinking	Inefficient practices due to lack of skill or processes
Fragmentation	Takes too much time
Duplication of processes and resources	Messy
Inefficient practices	Danger of group think
Expert blindness/tunnel vision	Wastes time
Tribalism/turf wars	Mistrust
Communication gaps/lags	Feeling evaluated
Innovation and creativity stifled	Not really collaboration
Mistrust	Power/authority by few (louder overpowers)
	Confusion
	Decisions not made/inaction

This is not a definitive list – you could add more!

Next step: Identify some ideas to leverage this polarity through action steps that allows us to *monitor and self-correct* as we go. Use the actions steps to keep on course and use the early warnings to adjust course as needed.

Silo Practices		Collaborative Practices	
Action Steps	Positive	Positive	Action Steps
Create a unified vision	Specialist knowledge	Shift from me to we	Create a unified vision for this polarity
Communicate and make links to the 'big picture' and how this team contributes to this	Contextualised and localised decision-making	Contributing to a common goal	Distribute leadership
Articulate and communicate common goals that align with whole-school goals	Efficiency	Inquiry and collective problem-solving approach	Communicate and make links to the 'big picture'
Make connections and links between specialist areas	Competitiveness between departments	Sharing practice, knowledge and problems	Articulate and communicate a common goal for the whole school
Create physical spaces for specialists to come together to share practices	Initiatives, resourcing and practices contextualised	Innovation as part of learning	Explicitly teach collaborative skills and processes
Teach and use conflict resolution skills	Operations specialised	Efficient	Teach and use conflict resolution skills
Mistakes are embraced for individual learning	Individual expertise promoted	Rich dialogue	Utilise specialist thinking to provide alternative ideas/solutions
Actively seek ideas that motivate individuals and specialist teams		Common language	Share practices across specialist areas
Actively seek, reflect and act on feedback		Value difference	Create physical spaces for collaboration to take place
		Promoting high levels of trust	Mistakes are embraced for collective learning
			Collective problem-solving
			Strong whole-school team culture
			Actively seek ideas that motivate and reward teams when working collaboratively

Early Warnings	Silo Practices Negative	Collaborative Practices Negative	Early Warnings
Fragmented ideas about vision and goals	Us and them thinking	Inefficient practices due to lack of skill or processes	Leadership not clear/mixed messages
Gate keeper mentality	Duplication of processes and resources	Takes too much time	Fragmented ideas about vision and goals
Rivalry between departments	Inefficient practices	Messy	Time poor
Practices outdated/failing to innovate	Expert blindness/tunnel vision	Danger of group think	One voice rather than many/too many voices
Time poor	Tribalism/turf wars	Wastes time	Diversity is not valued but criticised
Look to one person for 'answers'	Communication gaps	Mistrust	Processes are not efficient or in place
Practices and resources are not shared but protected	Fragmentation	Feeling evaluated	Absence of skills for collaborative practices
Diversity is not valued but criticised	Innovation and creativity stifled	Not really collaboration	Mistakes are viewed as individuals or teams as being less capable
People who are not willing to take risks	Mistrust	Power/authority by few (louder overpowers)	Risk taking is avoided for fear of criticism
Resources are duplicated		Confusion	Team culture resists change
Communication is funnelled		Decisions not made/inaction	Consistency does not allow for professional individualism
Tunnel vision			Feedback is not sought or acted upon
Consistency viewed as one-size-fits-all			
Feedback is not sought or acted upon			

Silo mentality as a construct of function, knowledge and experience

There are implications for policy, school systems and schools in the development of leadership partnered programs that envelop apprenticeship, job-embedded learning with dedicated time to learn. Leadership support and mentoring has to be foregrounded *in practice not just documents* and with emphasis on identification of 'assumed' knowledge, skills, experience that hinders and not assists in leading schools today. Contextualising this knowledge supports school leaders to strategically lead collaboration with the cognitive demands of sociality. Read Chapter 6 to delve into these ideas further.

Chapter 6

Implications for policy and practice

New to me
- Can I/we explain the implications for policy?
- Can I/we explain the implications for system leaders?
- Can I/we explain the implications for school leaders?
- Can I/we explain the implications for our context?

Revisiting, reviewing and revising familiar ideas
- Which aspects would I/we like to explore further? Why?
- In what ways do these implications, in this chapter, impact my/our context? How do you/we know?
- Can we explain my/our next steps?

Applying in unfamiliar, different or alternative contexts
- Which aspects of my/our knowledge from this chapter can we adapt or modify to suit my/our context?
- Why have I/we chosen these aspects?
- What key ideas will I/we need to be mindful of as I/we go about implementation?

Before you begin

The aim of this book is to share research that could support educators in their *intentional leadership of collaborative interactions* as a strategy for improvement, given:

- Theory that proposes limitations on the number of social contacts humans are equipped to handle (Dávid-Barrett & Dunbar, 2013; Dunbar et al., 2015; Mac Carron et al., 2016);
- The common organisation structures that educators operate within; and
- Considerations of day-to-day operational limitations (for example, competing demands on time, human and financial resources, short-term tasks that require immediate attention).

This chapter invites readers to *consider implications for leaders at all levels.*

Provocation

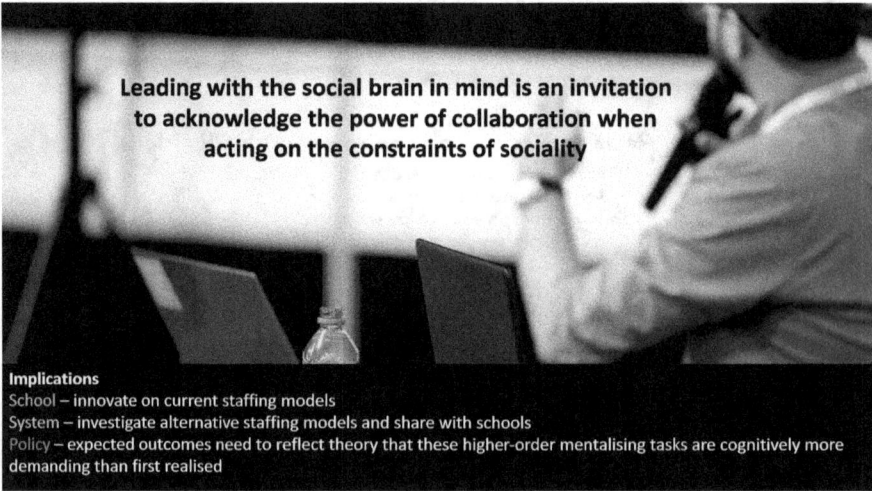

Leading with the social brain in mind is an invitation to acknowledge the power of collaboration when acting on the constraints of sociality

Implications
School – innovate on current staffing models
System – investigate alternative staffing models and share with schools
Policy – expected outcomes need to reflect theory that these higher-order mentalising tasks are cognitively more demanding than first realised

Questions to ponder

- How can school leaders strategically lead collaboration if there are possible cognitive limitations to interactions?

- If the average number of collaborative interactions for educators in schools, per week, is more than 150, what implications does this have for workload?
- How has the work in schools become more sophisticated?
- In what ways has policy accounted for the social and cognitive complexity of differentiated relationships when collaborating for student improvement?
- If silo mentality is promoted by school structures, the number and frequency of collaborative interactions required to undertake day-to-day work in schools, what are reasonable outcomes in the time available?

Leading collaboration requires deeper understandings about the associations between collaboration and silo mentality

Silo mentality

Collective wisdom

I began this book as the artificial intelligence explosion took off surrounding ChatGPT and applications that utilise language learning models. As I sit here writing this chapter, I am reminded of the numerous innovations that educators in schools contend with at each and every turn. At the same time of writing, I was prompted by someone in the same office that version 9 of the Australian Curriculum is now live. A brief (very) exploration (via the video) assured me that this version has been *designed by teachers for teachers* and is easily navigated. There are all kinds of resources to assist... including updates that I can subscribe to.

Is it any wonder that teachers and school leaders experience an increasing intensification of their work. With just these two 'innovations', educators will scramble to make sense of balancing the implications for curriculum and all that encompasses. I don't dare mention pedagogy! On their own each of these mean opportunities and constraints for individuals *and* teams. More specifically, as these individuals and teams work collaboratively to deliver the expectations that emerge from these 'new' initiatives, the cognitive demands can go unrecognised. Lost in a sea of other opportunities and constraints, distribution of the effort, attention and energy for those working in schools contributes to silo mentality as a self-protection mechanism.

The ideas and suggestions throughout this chapter acknowledge that silos and silo mentality, as an organisational metaphor, occur in organisations by design and by default. The study that was the catalyst for this book reinforced theories that these psychological and physical barriers are based on the mental and social models that, as humans, we classify and organise for specific purposes (Tett, 2016). Schools are structured and organised in specific ways and based on historical notions of efficiency and effectiveness in educating large numbers for specific purposes. Since the 1980s, collaboration has been embraced as a way to break down cultures of individualism (silo mentality) and isolationism (silos) within the teaching profession. Harnessing the potential for collective social capital within schools has and is an ongoing process with varying results. Research has investigated and theorised on the reasons for this. Each study contributes to our continuing understanding of the why, how, when and where collaboration works. Explorations also share the barriers to collaboration in school contexts.

> **Sarah (Head of Department):** "Trying to coordinate timetables across the school for people to get together is a nightmare."

Supporting leaders and teachers in their work means thinking about the phenomenon of silos in alternative ways. If we consider that this phenomenon is influenced by an individual's capacity to cognitively maintain a limited number of relationships at any one time and therefore, combined with the nature of complex organisations, then silos are a naturally occurring consequence and protective mechanism to deal with such chaos. Within a school context (and possibly in most organisations), chaos is not a description that is welcomed or viewed positively, and so I would like to reiterate that chaos is being defined as the unexpected shifts in the predictable. In a school context, you might hear some saying "well, that came out of left field" and yet others might say "you have got to be kidding, we planned on this *and* now you are telling me we must do this?" Adjust, switch, change, backflip, move to the side and you want it due when?

> **Angela (Classroom Teacher):** "All these mini groups that I belong to – and there are many – I am supposed to go back and share, [but there's] no time to do that in the four minutes I am given."

The type of collaborative work to improve student outcomes today involves a layering of multiple demands and expectations that necessitate numerous interactions, skills and processes being undertaken within limited time frames and using additional time and cognitive energy.

> **Sarah (Head of Department):** "There are just so many multi-levels of teams and collaboration and [that is] so *complex*, but [there is] more this year, moving forward with the new curriculum than ever before... And we would never have been able to move

those two teams together with all the *complexities* that come with moving two different teams into one... It makes it that much more *complex* – it's not just one or two people's role; it's now everybody's role to make sure that that's happening."

As a consequence, it is more likely that the inclination, ability or *mental space* to seek or see 'the big picture' or engage in systems thinking with a vision of the larger organisation is absent. While there can be arguments made that big-picture thinking is not necessary for everyone, I would argue that those working in complex organisations benefit from an overview of where things fit within the entire organisation, and this enables a variety of perspectives when thinking about situations, problems, decisions, teams or individuals. One problem, though, is that this type of thinking is difficult to access when working with limited knowledge of the organisation as a whole. At the same time, it is natural for leaders at all levels of education to operate *within their silos* and promote silo mentality without intention, but their decisions or inaction can lead to unintended consequences that can provide barriers for collaboration. What follows is not intended to eliminate silo mentality but rather, in light of research findings, support school leaders to challenge system leaders and policymakers in their assumptions about unintended costs when using collaboration as a strategy for school improvement.

Leading collaboration in schools requires understanding about the cognitive demands of sociality

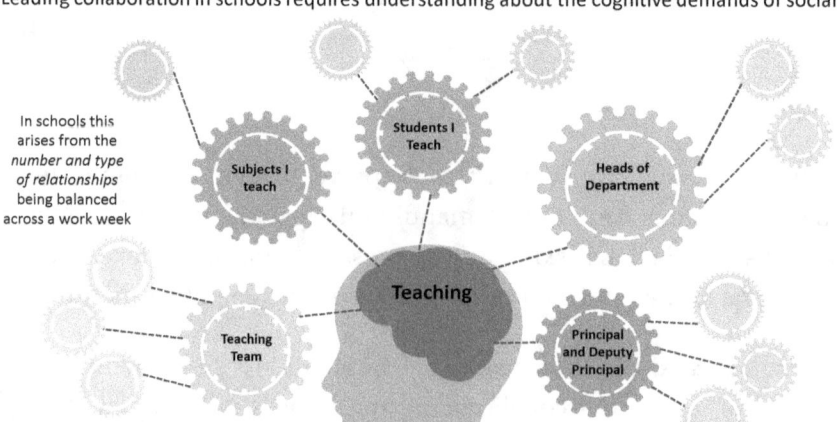

Education policy

To begin with, education policy documents may acknowledge that schools are complex organisations, but this is not reflected in practice. The reality is that policies carve up different pieces to focus on the parts and ignore *the sum of the components interwoven with intricate relationships between these components* (Devereux et al., 2020). Interpreting and enacting policy is difficult work, but there are assumptions that sit behind and within the documents themselves. Often there is little time in schools to examine connections and contradictions. The criticism here is developing policy is siloed. While enactment is contextualised within the broader education system and then more specifically each school, school leaders are overwhelmed with a tsunami of policies that offer possibilities but within the limitations and constraints of their context. The visible costs of translating policy into practice can be quantified, but the hidden costs are not always recognisable and therefore calculated. School leaders are abandoned by and with policy.

Additional and different types of knowledge, training and professional experience support the transition of leaders from one role to another. Yet, school leaders are expected to know what these are and how to access them. If the priorities of a school determine the allocation of resources and these are directed, in part by national and state policies relevant to their location, and in part by the values and focus of the school or local community, decisions about where best to invest time and resources can be a costly exercise. For example, leadership support and mentoring is evident in policy documents and in some systems foregrounded in practice, however, this can be seen as a financial burden on a school, rather than a long-term investment. At the same time, there can be an underlying assumption that 'support' for leaders means that they are not up to the job. Education policy has yet to acknowledge that leadership programs require investment in additional and different types of knowledge, training and professional experience to support school leaders in leading the type of collaboration required to improve student achievement.

Daniel (Head of Department): "I underestimated the people skills I would need to fulfil my responsibilities in leading and managing a department. That's not something you pick up as a teacher."

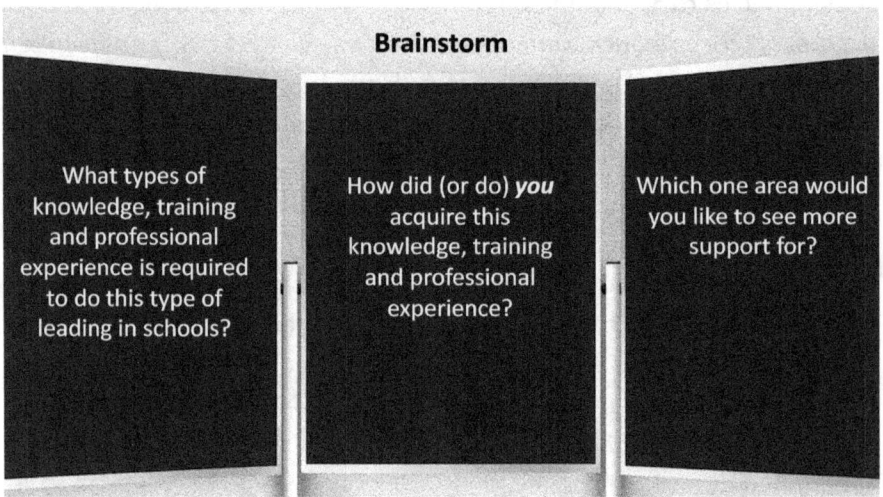

Brainstorm

What types of knowledge, training and professional experience is required to do this type of leading in schools?

How did (or do) *you* acquire this knowledge, training and professional experience?

Which one area would you like to see more support for?

Investing in the pathways for school leaders, at a policy level, in a cohesive and systematic way, can prioritise the development of people skills and, more specifically, knowledge required to maintain differentiated relationships that have become more cognitively demanding. Social complexity is necessary for the types of collaboration in schools and has gone unrecognised for the reason that specialist knowledge, skills and abilities are devalued in mechanistic and simplistic notions of implementation. Collaborating in school contexts is valuable and important work, but maintaining these types of relationships are cognitively demanding, since the effort, energy and attention necessary to deliver outcomes within limited time frames is currently underestimated. Educators balance a knowledge of content in addition to the cognition required to make meaning of social behaviours based on their personal constructs and integrate this in attempts to undertake tasks that may or may not get completed prior to moving to the next equally important task.

Kate (Head of Department): "I think the professional learning is kind of what you find for yourself… Nothing that I recall was drawn directly saying you have learned this leadership stuff, now apply it here. Hopefully, people picked up skills to apply there. But prior to that... nothing. Leadership through mentoring and modelling through our current admin has been strong and good. There have been courses that come out if you want to apply to learn how to do interviews and to write resumes and that sort of stuff – nothing focused on leadership unless you're motivated yourself to learn how to be a leader. It's not going to happen."

Policymakers are invited to explicitly bridge gaps that have arisen over time in the absence of foregrounding schools as organisations with human relationships at the core of their work. Without contextualising policy in this way, interpretations, implementation and enactment become a series of inputs and outputs with a cause-effect reductionist approach. We have seen how this plays out over and over in schools.

The emphasis and investment focus on initial teacher education and the continued professional learning of teachers is evident in policy, but now, more than ever, it is imperative to support school leaders more proactively. Marsh et al. (2022) describe the increasing urgency that faces schools to replace leaders with suitable candidates. Policies that advocate for practical measures and resources in preparing and continuing to assist school leaders to meet the demands of their roles and job characteristics are not a luxury, or a nice to have – they are non-negotiable necessity!

Leoni (Executive Principal): "That's one of the things that sticks in my mind – the transition for principals over the years. Completing your first year is probably joyous. Your second year, you're starting to decipher where it is and what it is you're doing. Your third year, you're starting to go holy [expletive], this is hard. This change agenda is hard. And your third or fifth year, in my opinion, is where you see the unravelling. And those guys are the ones that really need support! Maybe we can get to them before they unravel. But you have got to have a relationship. You can send out the SWAT team but those teams need to have people who are able to build a relationship really, really quickly."

Three areas for policy to speak to are:

1. *Leading schools requires additional and different types of knowledge, training and professional experience* mirroring increased intensification of work in schools as *complex organisations*. Understanding *organisation theory* that is more *specifically nuanced* for these types of organisations is a necessity.

2. Leading collaboration demands deeper understandings about the *associations between collaboration and silo mentality and how these are influenced by an organisation's structure*. Explicitly encouraging education leaders in their efforts to *use holistic thinking when recognising and addressing silo mentality as a construct of function, knowledge and experience* is a process, not a destination. Promoting *partnerships with inside-outside boundary-crossing mentors* to address *one silo being cocooned by another* can be an important contribution to this process.

3. Investigations into *current and alternative staffing models* that can and do *allocate time* for collaborative interactions *within the workday* signify the influence that *social complexity has on those that work in school contexts*. Consequently, expectations of educators need to be reasonable given considerations for *time available, differentiated relationships, the number of relationships and increases in the intensity of teachers' and leaders' work today*.

Education systems

Leadership pathways, in Australia, mostly represent an apprenticeship model. Historically, becoming a leader in a school meant that you moved through the 'ranks' – from teacher to middle leader to senior leader. While there may be variations to this pathway, the inclusion of formal qualifications is not necessarily a prerequisite. I have heard that becoming a leader in a school can be described in one of three ways: appointed, anointed or accidental.

> **Daniel (Head of Department):** "You don't get your diploma of being a Head of Department. It's an apprenticeship – coming up through being a teacher. I'm not the best with having initiatives. I'm much better responding to and developing skills as I'm called to. My boss saw strengths in me, asked me to get into student management and behaviour management – which is something I always said I wouldn't do. I was then approached to apply for the Head of Department position. I said, I would definitely not do that one. And then the boss encouraged me to go that way."

> **Angela (Classroom Teacher):** "I had never acted as a Head of Department. I started here in 2000 and never had any acting positions. I'm not a Head of Department of a Faculty. I'm a Head of Department Senior Schooling and Vet. So, it's different again, and there was no one who had previously been in that position. They created that position."

While I am not suggesting that formal qualifications are necessary, I am wondering if this pathway offers the necessary knowledge or experience to lead in the current educational landscape. I would also argue that this pathway, alone, places huge burdens on school leaders to equip themselves with knowledge, experience and skill sets within the increasing demands of their day-to-day work. Given that research touts the importance that school leaders play in student improvement (even if indirectly), is it equitable that leaders are coming to this work feeling ill-prepared or worse, left to *pick up* what you *think you need* along the way?

> **Richard (Head of Department):** "I'd have to go and find PD [professional development] because I thought I needed that, or

I'd have to source some further skills in post educational studies. Usually this was after someone had made reference to them [skills] elsewhere or pointed them out to me."

This is an ad hoc and haphazard approach that misses opportunities to develop leadership partnership programs that *envelop apprenticeship, job-embedded learning* with *dedicated time* to learn. These types of programs can support education leaders in becoming interactional practitioners and theorists who use panoramic views and multiple perspectives to develop their understanding of what is taking place in their contexts. Interactional practitioners, as theorists, centre relationships at the heart of the work being undertaken in schools. More specifically, as they lead collaboration, rich dialogue becomes the foundation for shaping decisions. Honouring the time and the people within this work says much about collective values and beliefs of those within the system.

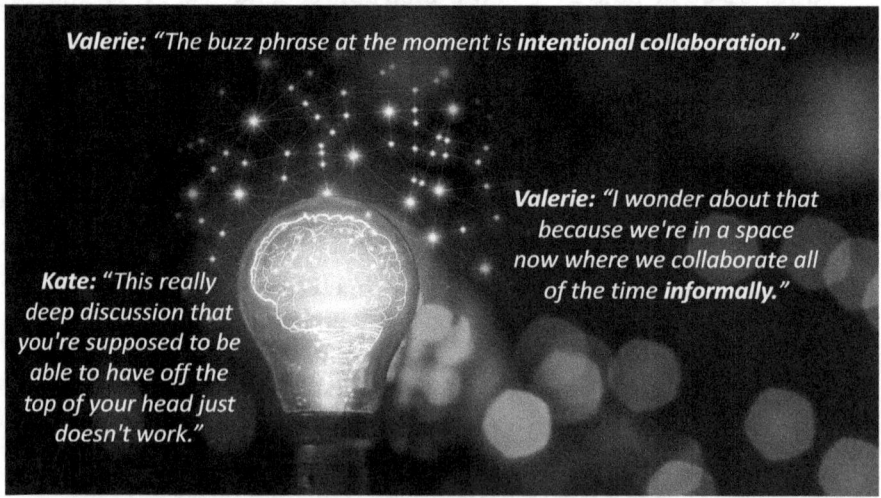

Valerie: "The buzz phrase at the moment is **intentional collaboration**."

Kate: "This really deep discussion that you're supposed to be able to have off the top of your head just doesn't work."

Valerie: "I wonder about that because we're in a space now where we collaborate all of the time **informally**."

In building theories for why things work, or don't work, leaders invest in their own professional learning. However, this cannot be accomplished with mixed messages coming from each education system (Government, Catholic and Independent). It is incumbent for leaders at a system level to actively remove barriers for school leaders to access and engage in professional learning that strengthens their individual and collective understanding in designing and structuring collaboration contextually as a strategy for improvement. One way to do this is exploring alternative staffing models that allows for *explicit adjustments* and *expectations* of educators given social brain theory being applied in school contexts.

As previously stated, social brain theory contends that there is a limit to the number of relationships that an individual can maintain. Yet, in a recent study, participants on average went above this limit on a weekly basis in undertaking their day-to-day work. Social complexity highlights the cognitive demands associated with maintaining these differentiated relationships that use higher-order mentalising tasks and yet this has not yet been considered with increases in the intensity of teachers' and leaders' work today. Structuring collaborative interactions is influenced by a leader understanding the reasonableness of outcomes, given the distribution of energy, attention and effort among different types and numbers of collaborative interactions given the available time.

Without alternative staffing models and modified expectations for collaborative interactions, the intensification of an educator's work will continue to be unreasonable in the time available within current organisational structures. Staffing models need to be reimagined to make the best use of the resources available. However, this assumes leaders, their mentors (if they have them) or their teams are equipped with *the necessary prior knowledge* and *experience to lead, manage and innovate for change* for *today's education landscape*. That is, what resources do they have available and what does it mean to make the best use of them? How do they know?

> **Ramona (Head of Department):** "...because when you're fumbling through something, you don't always find the best way."
>
> **Valerie (Campus Principal):** "That was an important day because one of the DPs (Deputy Principal) particularly had said to me previously that she had had no professional learning outside of school since she's been in that school, or since a previous school."

At the same time, it means that system leaders need to understand that silo mentality is a naturally occurring phenomena that shares characteristics that can be both advantageous and problematic for individuals and organisations. Therefore, it is essential that system and school leaders today are able to recognise when excessively insular mindset or mentality, including their own, shape and misshape behaviours and ways of working that inhibit collaboration as a strategy for school improvement. In practice, this means that leaders at all levels of the organisation are required to seek and communicate reasonable outcomes that consider misconstrued and underdiscussed aspects of implementing collaboration contextually as a strategy for school improvement. More specifically, system leaders are key supports in advocating for school leaders' continued professional learning.

> **Dianne (Classroom Teacher):** "There would be very few administrative staff when you look at the Deputy Principal or Principal level who have been a full-time teacher in a classroom for the better part of a decade. So, I think that their recollection of what it's like to be a full-time classroom teacher is based on what happened… when things were very different, they've changed so much… But I think that they don't actually get how complex some people's work is within what they are expected to do."

School leaders

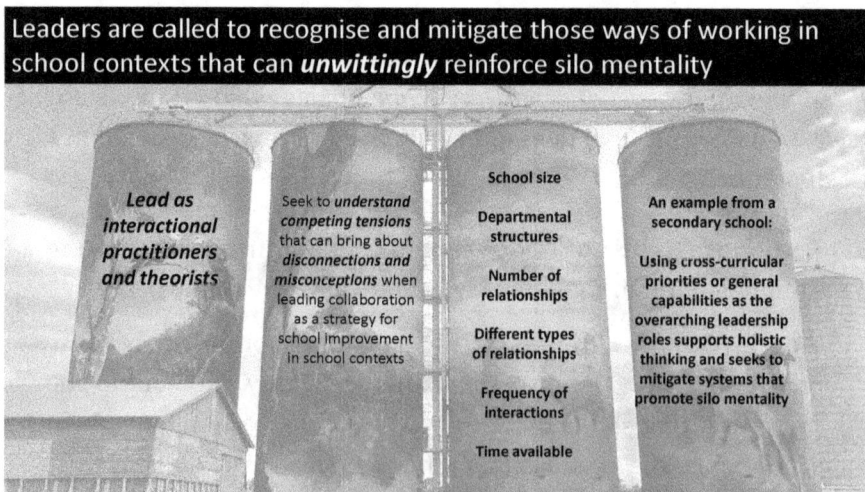

Silo mentality and collaboration are polarities that naturally create competing tensions for school leaders. Without additional and different types of knowledge, training and professional experience, school leaders are reliant on their apprenticeship pathway to lead, manage and innovate for change. This is no longer sufficient, as it produces silos cocooned within silos. Recognising and understanding the types of silo mentality operating at different levels in and across schools often takes 'boundary-crossing' individuals to *see and describe* the advantages and disadvantages more readily. Boundary crossing in this sense is defined as moving between, among or across functions, knowledge and experience. For example, some individuals work within different education sectors (Education QLD, Catholic Education or Independent System), within different sectors of schools (Primary, Junior Secondary, Senior Secondary), across different subject departments (Learning Support, Student Services), within different roles across different schools in different contexts (large schools, small schools, leadership, teaching, regional appointments) – and they seek out opportunities to build knowledge and relationships in crossing boundaries that naturally occur in schools. The value that these boundary-crossers bring to the organisation is a panoramic view that strives to utilise and develop the expertise of the organisation – with a range of resources within and beyond its borders. In essence, silo mentality can be recognised, challenged and addressed:

- **As a construct of function** where school leaders can be encouraged to explore overarching leadership roles that support holistic organisational thinking that seeks to mitigate systems that promote silo mentality. For example, revisiting role descriptions and responsibilities to determine purpose. Leaders can inherit roles and responsibilities that suit a different time and place.
- **As a construct of knowledge** where school leaders pause, ponder and pave way for co-constructed understandings for key concepts.
- **As a construct of experience** where school leaders acknowledge and value diversity of experiences to enrich initiatives.

School leadership is a tricky and contested field. The number of leadership styles that are described and promoted continues to grow. I would be surprised if you had not come across some of these: Instructional, Distributive, Transformational, Hierarchical and Authoritative. Irrespective of the ones you are familiar or unfamiliar with, all of them are underpinned by certain values and beliefs. However, school leaders don't always get opportunities to unpack these in relation to their work. Depending upon the focus for a system, leaders can find themselves with rhetoric handed to them (in policy documents) for a particular approach and style, but with inadequate scaffolds and practical application suitable for their contexts. It is then left to individuals and teams to make sense as they muddle along. The interesting piece is that throughout these, leaders theorise about why things are or aren't working, based on what they are witnessing in practice. Evidence is collected and what happens next depends on a leader understanding the nature of complex organisations. Competing tensions are part and parcel of complex organisations.

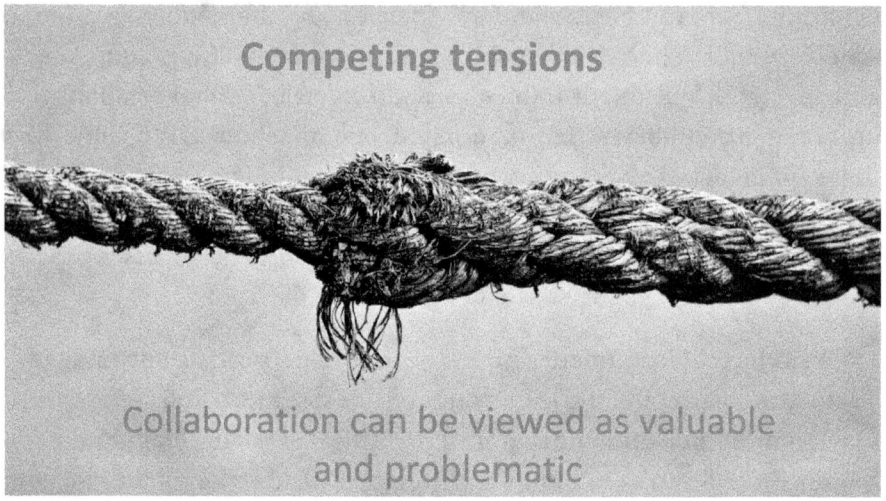

What this means is that leading as interactional practitioners and as theorists can reduce inherent gaps that come about with imagined realities. Disconnections and misconnections can be disrupted when school leaders work with theoretical and practical knowledge of complex organisations to inform decision-making processes. This intentional leadership is a result of investing in your own learning as well as the learning of others and includes designated time to identify 'assumed' knowledge, skills and experience. For example, structuring collaborative interactions is influenced by a leader understanding the *reasonableness of outcomes*, given the distribution of energy, attention and effort among different types and numbers of collaborative interactions given the available time. Time allocated, frequency of interaction, reciprocal trust, content knowledge and understanding of another's mindset all contribute to the social complexity of these interactions intended to improve student achievement.

Additionally, leading *and* managing can be conflated as a consequence of historical perceptions of designated positional roles and locked into particular ways of working. Imagining that schools cannot work in any other way can indicate siloed mentality.

> **Daniel (Head of Department):** "I think it has to be – I like the idea of having subject-specific faculties. I don't think you could ever lose that. That's the benefit of high school... you can take a Science pathway and in senior school you can take a trade pathway. There needs to be those options for the kids."

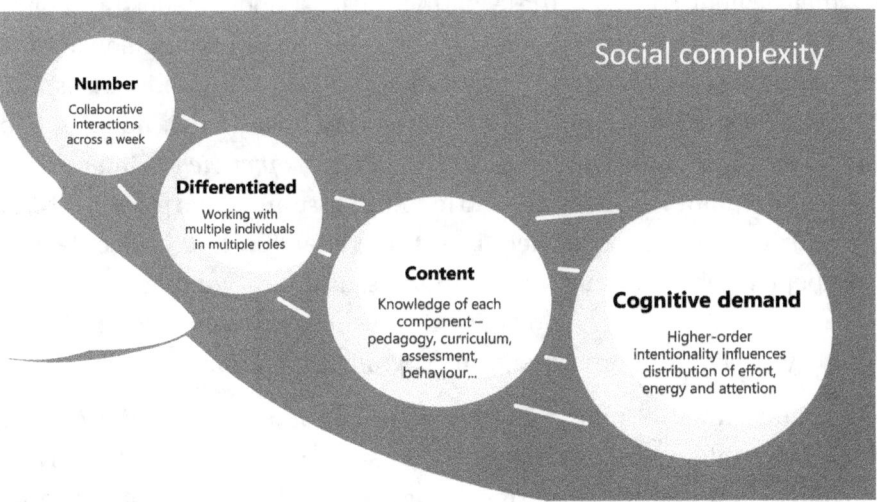

There can be a sense that certain organisation characteristics need to remain the same and the possibility of addressing some aspects viewed as unlikely because it does not serve preconceived worldviews of schools and schooling. In turn, this can influence promotional pathways that perpetuate leadership roles that reflect silo mentality as a construct of function. The loss of discipline integrity can be a fear that operates implicitly and explicitly and can have far-reaching implications in the short and long term. Specialist knowledge and expertise is powerful in its potential and should not be disregarded or abandoned. However, designing leadership teams that maintain the integrity of discipline knowledge and expertise with boundary-crossing purposes can encourage dialogue and problem-solving from multiple and diverse perspectives. Silos can be leveraged for collective wisdom! Structuring collaborative interactions for the purpose of student improvement involves knowledge *and* experience with expertise in content, process, product and environment for all. Yet, valuing and tapping into the wisdom of others is challenging when combined with expectations for current workloads.

School leaders can be 'trapped' within silos of knowledge and experience that (mis)shape responses to these problems of practice. Partnering with universities or other education providers to *employ inside-outside boundary-crossing mentors* offers opportunities to explore silo mentality in their school contexts. These partners can support leadership teams and contribute to conversations that promote more panoramic views of the specific school context. They are able to encourage individuals and teams to move across areas of the organisation, scanning, noticing and wondering how pieces fit and don't fit. This *helicopter view* is intended to give opportunities to *hover over* and identify those areas that require further investigation. The purpose here is to bring attention to those contextual competing tensions that arise from associations among a school's organisational structure, the ways in which collaboration is used as a strategy for school improvement, and cognitive limitations for interactions.

It is important to note that the addition of an *insider-outsider* or knowledgeable other (Sharratt, 2019) is specifically selected to provide ongoing support and mentoring for leaders and therefore needs to be *someone outside the system*. Being *outside the system* brings a sense of trust that is paramount and largely connected to perceptions of influence. Being open to work with a mentor and what is revealed is dependent on an individual being seen as not sitting in 'judgement' or influencing (positively or negatively) promotional opportunities. Yet, it is essential that this partner has insider knowledge and understanding of schools as organisations today. Developing trust within these partnerships begins with the selection of a partner who has credibility based on experience, extensive knowledge and relationship building.

Helicopter view
– Moving across
– Scanning
– Seeking things that stand out or don't fit
– Noticing and wondering

Simon (Deputy Principal): "I think Principals need courage to look beyond their own system for support. It's fair to say that the person we reached out to was someone we knew and trusted. Her skills are quite unique. It would be difficult to duplicate somebody of her quality and fit for our context. In other words, the Principal and I sought a professional mentor for the leadership team."

Lilly (Deputy Principal): "We are in professional mentorship with someone who we trust and has incredible knowledge. This has been instrumental in how we have developed our roles and the learning that sits with collaboration with multiple teams. I have never got that anywhere else. I would say the master's that I did spoke about it in theory, but I think what we've got here is quite rare."

Conclusion

Education policy and systems have fallen short in their efforts to adequately prepare, develop and support school leader pathways in developing additional and different types of knowledge, training and professional experience in cohesive and ongoing ways. Valuing opportunities to redefine what is reasonable in the time available when using collaboration within the school structures of a school leader's context is absent. This highlights possibilities for leaders to restructure using *boundary crossing* as a mechanism for creating panoramic views of departmental silos. This can also be employing an *insider-outsider* as one school leader did for the very purpose of shifting insular focus among leadership teams.

This brings attention to preparation and pathways for those moving into leadership roles and the ongoing support for those in leadership roles today. *Leading schools requires additional and different types of knowledge, training and professional experience* than what can be provided by apprenticeship models alone. Assuming prior knowledge and experience is enough to lead, manage and innovate for change adds to constraints when employing collaboration as a strategy for school improvement in secondary school contexts.

Apprenticing can promote silo mentality because leaders are *created in the image* of those they have been mentored by. In this study, participants discussed the advantages and disadvantages of this. However, what was consistent was the inconsistency of the experience, skills and training for leaders – those aspiring to become them and those that had been in the role for many years. Some continued to expand their knowledge, skills and experiences beyond the school silo, but others viewed this learning as taking away from valuable time on-site. Thus, professional learning for leaders can be fragmented and based on the various components that make up day-to-day operations of the school, particularly in the age of measurement (Biesta, 2017a).

Reducing this complex system to the sum of its many parts encourages leaders to pursue professional learning dependent on the current focus for continuous school improvement (Glen et al., 2017) and assume that each of these parts exists in isolation (Devereux et al., 2020) or replace and substitute what has come before. While leaders have access to various professional learning, this mechanistic approach highlights how there can be such disparity among the types of leader knowledge, skill, experience and training. Focusing on the many parts, without actively and deliberately supporting leaders to make connections among intricate relationships between the parts, can amplify the chaos and unpredictability of working in complex organisations (Devereux et al., 2020). Therefore, continuous school improvement must consider how leaders are supported to develop, enrich, enhance or ultimately challenge their current experience, skills, knowledge and training when leading complex organisations such as secondary schools. In considering future preparation and support of school leaders, it is important to redress notions that self-learning takes away from valuable time on-site.

Mapping next steps

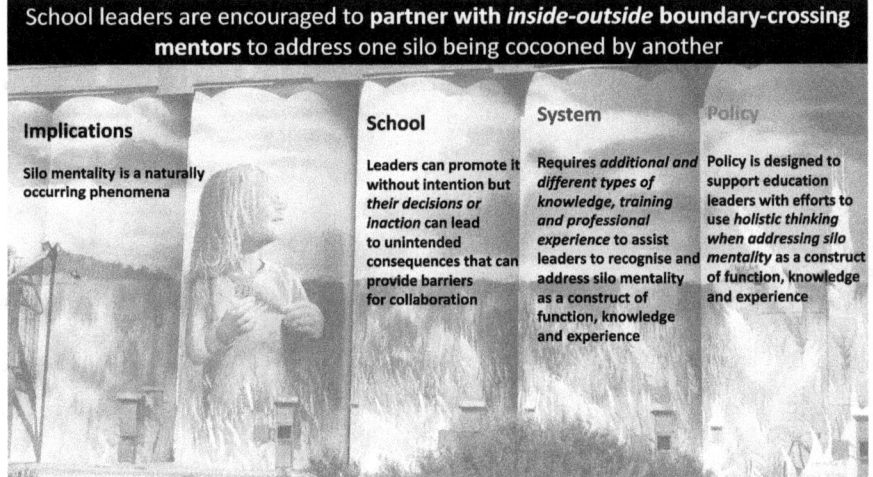

School leaders are encouraged to **partner with *inside-outside* boundary-crossing mentors** to address one silo being cocooned by another

Implications

Silo mentality is a naturally occurring phenomena

School

Leaders can promote it without intention but their decisions or inaction can lead to unintended consequences that can provide barriers for collaboration

System

Requires *additional and different types of* knowledge, training and professional experience to assist leaders to recognise and address silo mentality as a construct of function, knowledge and experience

Policy

Policy is designed to support education leaders with efforts to use *holistic thinking* when addressing silo *mentality* as a construct of function, knowledge and experience

- Where will you adjust leadership programs to reflect understandings that leadership apprenticing is important but not sufficient for today's education landscape?
- List examples of alternative staffing models that apply social brain theory to the work in school contexts.
- Who might be someone that can act as an *insider-outsider* to observe and provide feedback? A pair of neutral eyes may see what we are blind to!

Chapter 7

Mapping situational context with Wardley Mapping

New to me
- Can I/we explain what it means to create systems for greater situational awareness, including self-awareness and being knowledgeable of the components of the work we lead?
- What does it mean to lead with emotional intelligence and build cohesion with social intelligence? Why is this important for school leaders?
- What is a Wardley Map and why would I/we create one?

Revisiting, reviewing and revising familiar ideas
- Which systems and processes do I/we have in place to create greater situational awareness?
- What do I/we need to be more knowledgeable in?
- What examples can I/we identify as leading with emotional and social intelligence?
- How might a Wardley Map help us further?

Applying in unfamiliar, different or alternative contexts
- Which aspects of my/our knowledge from this chapter can I/we adapt or modify to suit my/our context?
- Why have I/we chosen these aspects?
- What key ideas will I/we need to be mindful of as I/we go about implementation?

Before you begin

Australian school-improvement agendas are continuously responding to what is perceived as declining academic performance jeopardising the attainment of Australia's aspiration for excellence and equity in school education. Yet, *educators within schools are working harder than ever!* This chapter invites you to consider an *alternative way* to represent your situational context in relation to the initiatives you are employing for school improvement.

Provocation

> "If initiative overload and fragmentation are keeping your best plans from becoming reality, it's time to start leading differently."
>
> – FULLAN & QUINN, 2016

Questions to ponder

- What tensions exist for you as a leader in your context?
- If self-awareness, emotional and social intelligence are considered 'soft skills', why are they so hard in practice?
- How can Leading with a Social Brain in Mind support a school leader's work?
- Can you describe the leadership styles or models that resonate for you?
- What does it look, feel and sound like to lead in this way?
- Do your staff know this? How do you know?

Create systems for greater self-awareness

The *Australian Professional Standard for Principals and the Leadership Profiles* describe the knowledge, understanding and expectations for succeeding in their work. Leaders are very much aware that their position, roles and responsibilities require them to know their strengths and own their areas for growth. This is not at issue. The pace and urgency of multiple demands in schools is. Day-to-day operations allow little time for self-reflection and, if there is time, this type of investment can be viewed as indulgent, unnecessary or competition to other more important work. Creating systems for greater self-awareness is vital in leading schools as complex organisations.

Leading with the Social Brain in Mind situates leaders in ways that proactively makes connections to the additional and different types of knowledge, experience and skills necessary for workplaces with the *'layering' of multiple demands and expectations requiring numerous interactions, skills and processes undertaken within limited time frames and using additional time and cognitive energy.* The enemy, in many cases for leaders, is time, not an unwillingness to engage in this type of work. Their own capacity is impacted by the number and differentiated relationships that their role requires. Making choices in when, how and why they distribute their energy, effort and attention impacts the capacity for reform, organisational learning and social capital both on an organisational and individual level. It is not something that is broken or needs to be fixed! Acceptance brings forth possibilities for the way we think about schools as organisations and compels educators to evaluate workloads and expected outcomes in the time available.

Schools rely on the concept of silos to maintain efficiency for the day-to-day running of operations. Many leaders are excellent managers of operations, but unfortunately, this may not always support the effectiveness of an improvement agenda. In some cases, leaders may have a very different view of how the improvement agenda is going compared to those who are undertaking the 'improvement'. Have you ever heard leaders described in these ways: "He doesn't have a clue"; "She thinks everything is running smoothly but the ship is sinking"; "They have lost touch with what it is like to be in a classroom"; "Morale around here is at an all-time low".

Leaders who actively engage in 'warts and all' dialogue will seek feedback from a range of people (yes, especially those ones we might try to avoid from time to time!). The purpose is to obtain a richer, more fine-grained picture of the perceptions of the work they believe they are leading. This also includes the implementation process. *How does your leadership of this work look, feel and sound like to others? How is the implementation of the key agendas going?* In an age of accountability and, more importantly, reflective practice, we need to ensure our leaders have the same opportunities as our students and teachers do, in seeking and receiving feedback. The gap between perceptions and current reality then becomes the work needed to align and to minimise silo operations that may derail improvement agendas.

Be knowledgeable

Is it reasonable to ask our leaders to be experts in all aspects of their work? I don't believe so, nor do I think there is an expectation for them to be. Being 'knowledgeable' is not the same as being an expert, but there have been times when I feel that they have been used interchangeably in school contexts. It is why I wish to distinguish between the two here.

'Expertise' refers to a depth of understanding with high levels of skill, experience and practice in a specific field, whereas being 'knowledgeable' is a more general understanding of a subject or particular area. School leaders need to be knowledgeable in the areas identified as key improvement agendas. Too many times we see leaders who are asking teachers to implement practices without a contextual and realistic understanding of the practicalities for implementation.

A leader's past teaching experience can be remembered through rose-coloured glasses. The distance (geographically and the passing of time) between classroom and leadership roles shapes and misshapes what a leader will imagine can and can't be accomplished in the time available. The *past imagined reality* can clash with a *current imagined reality*, particularly when these experiences are used to inform decisions without the benefit of seeing interconnected parts. Being knowledgeable means learning and working alongside and with their teaching teams, not being absent either physically or mentally. It also might mean that we take another hard look at the items on the improvement agenda and make decisions about the urgency and importance of each. Too many times teachers are being asked to implement a range of 'priorities' even the best of educators would find problematic. Teachers feel overwhelmed and pulled in too many directions to give dedicated focus to multiple agendas. Silos compartmentalise thinking and, consequently, improvement strategies will be viewed as separate and isolated agendas that cannot possibly be given the time and energy that they deserve. Leaders need to consider how the 'pieces' for improvement are interrelated and which ones to prioritise. Then, dedicate time, effort and focus for human and financial resources.

Lead with emotional intelligence

> "Seventy-five per cent of careers are derailed for reasons related to emotional competencies, including inability to handle interpersonal problems; unsatisfactory team leadership during times of difficulty or conflict; or inability to adapt to change or elicit trust."
>
> – THE CENTER FOR CREATIVE LEADERSHIP

Research indicates that the power and impact emotional intelligence has on organisational change, innovation and improvement is significant. School leaders are all too aware of the impact that change has on staff. However, this does not always mean that leaders address the obvious – change affects people in different ways and their reactions demonstrate this. Too many times change can be met with resistance or apathy, and there have been times where I have seen individuals or groups pretending to embrace change with a smile and all the cooperation in the world, but with nothing being done at the classroom level. Ignoring change or hoping that staff will just get used to the changes being implemented can and will undermine the change efforts.

If we wish to be cost-effective, then spend the time, effort and funds to put measures in place to build your own emotional intelligence and that of the teams we work with. The key message here is to build effective communication skills with and between *all* staff and understand how difference is a good thing and adds value to the organisation and each other personally. Silos ensure like-minded people gravitate towards each other. This can mean pockets of greatness, support for improvement or discontent and dissension. Rather than being frustrated with differences in reactions, embrace them as feedback on next steps or issues to consider! Leading with emotional intelligence means seeing difference as an asset and resource to the organisation – not something that needs to be conformed or removed.

Build cohesion with social intelligence

> "The most fundamental discovery of this new science:
> We are wired to connect."
>
> – DANIEL GOLEMAN

Relationships, relationships, relationships! The "new science" Daniel Goleman is referring to is neuroscience and, in this case, how our social interactions play a role in reshaping our brain. These interactions take on deep consequence as we realise how, through their total, we create one another. That is, emotions are contagious! If we think about this at a school level and implementing change agendas, the question becomes: What is being created through the social interactions required to engage in change efforts in your context? "Socially intelligent leaders start with being fully present and getting in sync" (Goleman, 2006). Is rapport being built with and among teams to carry out the work? Currently, collaboration is a key driver within schools. Unfortunately, just because we ask people to collaborate doesn't mean that it will just happen or happen effectively. It is important to ensure that the skills and processes are put in place to support the relationship building within teams.

As a leader, are you tuned into the issues of implementation within your context? Are you looking for ways that will allow voice and choice in the improvement agenda implementation? Therefore, being socially intelligent is not just being intelligent about our own relationships, but also within them. As previously stated – silos promote like-mindedness. At its worst, it can become toxic and derail teamwork and collaborative intentions.

Situating your context with Wardley Mapping

Strategic planning is not new in schools and leaders invest vast amounts of resources in developing various approaches to undertake this work. The success of these different approaches will depend on who you ask. Needless to say, planning strategically is a lot of work that usually results in documents detailing the work to be done. Not always, but for efficiency and consistency school systems and school leaders will provide planning templates, examples and models that can be borrowed, copied and adapted. What seems like a time-saving solution actually lacks an authentic way to *conceptualise the landscape* (a specific school context) that these educators work. At the same time, these documents can be intended to align different departments, functions and groups across a school, but this is not always the case.

In fact, these documents can promote isolation (silo mentality) because of the policy focus or the agenda being addressed. It can be too easy to dismiss an agenda if you don't think it applies to you or your department. A Wardley Map can help with alignment issues within and between groups because it helps individuals see the whole. It can be used in a way that everyone can talk about the same space with the same instrument. Creating and using a Wardley Map can be a powerful way to explore and explain school-improvement initiatives at a contextual level.

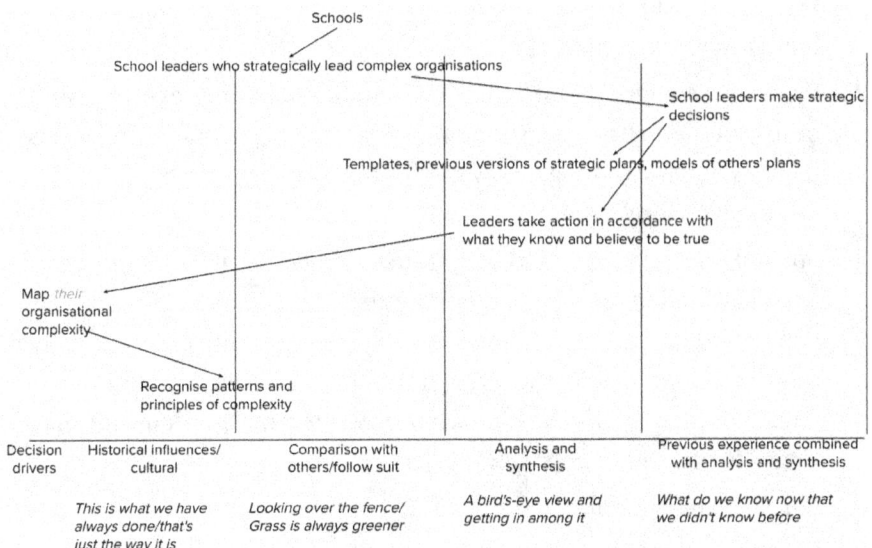

Wardley Mapping example

I first came across Simon Wardley, creator of Wardley Mapping (learnwardleymapping.com) during my PhD journey. As I watched some of his talks, read his book, listened to podcasts and took a 'course' (thank you, Ben Mosior, at *Hired Thought,* hiredthought.com), I became curious about the possibilities that his mapping technique might offer educators in schools. Although excited, I was cautious about using a technique developed by a strategist and business consultant from the other side of the world. Although his credentials are impressive, it was the extensive use of Wardley Maps *in business* that concerned me. The characteristics of schools are unlike other forms of organisations. Transplanting a technique from business, without contextualising for schools (as organisations), has not always worked in the past and I did not want to contribute more noise and confusion for school leaders developing strategy, strategic visions and annual operation plans. Yet, there were several things that resonated and offered possibilities in addressing issues that arise for educators in school contexts. Specifically, where to invest time, attention, effort and energy when confronted with multiple demands vying for the same limited resources.

The aspects that were transferable from a business organisation to a school were:

1. Wardley Mapping is a *process*.
2. It is *context specific*.
3. It uses a *visual technique* to understand that all things evolve over time and their characteristics change (systems, products, processes). If characteristics change, how might this assist leaders with decision-making?
4. *Position of components* of the system or process can be identified and classified in terms of their evolution and how they are connected. This seemed useful in anticipating where different groups might stall or move forward. (Evolutionary Characteristics Cheat Sheet adapted by Ben Mosior is a useful reference for determining stages for school contexts.)
5. *Patterns* are evident.
6. Opportunities for improvement can be identified/*challenged* or better understood.

Further explorations provided me with an opportunity to be part of an education mapping research working group with Simon. I quickly realised that I required additional and different types of knowledge. I was familiar with an education silo – Australian Schools, Higher Education, but this group of individuals was from different parts of the UK, Italy, Switzerland, Germany, the United States, India and Australia. Some were in Higher Ed, business and vocational, and many had backgrounds in technology. Familiarity with Wardley Mapping was varied. Although we were *all* talking about education and using similar terms, we were operating from different experiences, skill sets and knowledge – and those labels we attached to concepts had different meanings.

There were also different terms being used for the same concepts. But there were terms that I was unfamiliar with *because* I didn't have a background in the business world or technology. I spent time looking up phrases and terms over the time we were together (GitHub, Devos, blockchain, Miro) so that I could make sense of what we were discussing. At times, I felt way out of my depth and wondered what on earth I had gotten myself into! But I kept going back because of the people and the opportunity I suspected this was affording me – a chance to break out of my silo and boundary cross. Group norms for interacting were clearly established at the start of the process. Expectations were outlined for our fortnightly, one-hour, online get-together. I observed a gradual release of responsibility over time, and I could see the potential advantages for school and system leaders to use Wardley Maps in their own contexts.

It is important to point out that there are some disadvantages to using Wardley Mapping. Firstly, a map can have little meaning for those not part of the process. I shared one map that our group had created with the colleague who had first introduced me to Wardley Mapping, and our conversation highlighted the assumed understanding that was attached to different components of the map. I witnessed this during sessions with our group when individuals had missed sessions. I also witnessed the expert quickly read through a map, check for, and seek confirmation, of understanding. This is important. Remember, maps may be difficult to interpret if people do not understand the components of the system and how they interact with each other, but we can also assume understanding when they do.

Next, visualising an entire system in one map can be difficult. A single map can become overcrowded with information and then identifying patterns in the data is challenging. Alternatively, maps can lack detail that make subtle changes in the system hard to identify, too. Lastly, Wadley Mapping is a *tool* not a *solution*. It allows for assumptions to be challenged and questions to be asked in a safe space. It is a means of communication and represents a moment in time; reality is always changing, and so a map's value lies in revisiting, updating and adjusting the map to reflect the current context.

As we have seen in previous chapters, the expertise that makes silos a strength can also mean that silo mentality can narrow the focus of vision. What is visible to some may not be visible to others and this can depend on how 'close' you are to the situation. The needs or components for a change initiative and the capabilities to make that happen may not be *visible* to those who are not directly affected on a day-to-day basis. Positioning the relationships and creating links among and between them goes a long way in supporting individuals and groups to understand what has and hasn't been considered. My experience in working in school contexts with this tool points to value in different groups negotiating *visibility* of key capabilities and what that means for day-to-day operations and classroom practice.

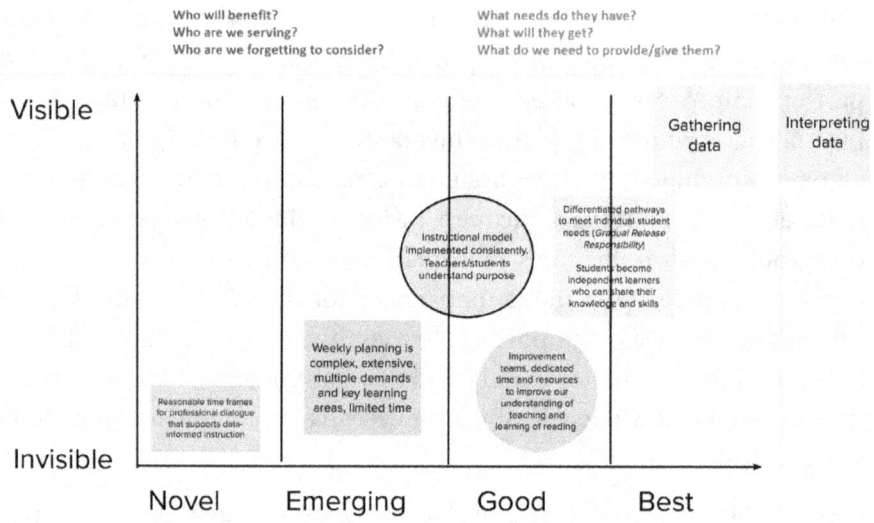

Create a Wardley Map as your next step to visualise the *Big Picture* and how the pieces fit together.

1. List improvement agenda/s that are taking place throughout your school.
2. Brainstorm terms associated with these agendas.
3. Identify the necessary parts (components) for each agenda to be successful.
4. Determine relationships. How are these parts connected or how do they interact with each other? (What depends on what? What is needed for this to occur?)
5. Position the components on a map. Horizontal axis = Determine where they sit on the evolutionary scale (four stages); Vertical Scale = Determine where they are in terms of visibility. Closer to the top more visible to the user (the individuals/groups benefitting).
6. Use the map to determine where we will invest our energy, effort and attention to move this forward.

Getting the map 'right' or 'perfect' is not the purpose of this process. The intent is to create a map (or maps) that visualises *your context* and provides insights into underlying assumptions that influence decision-making processes.

Conclusion

Leading collaboration is a complex task within a school and more so in contexts with many institutional structures and practices so taken for granted that they are rarely challenged. Ignoring or being unaware of the implications, or applications, of social brain theory for leading collaboration as a strategy for improvement can impact the success of the strategy and underestimate its costs to those directly involved. Creating systems for self-awareness encourages leaders to identify and advocate additional and different types of knowledge, experience and skills necessary within their own contexts. Being knowledgeable is not the same as having expertise, but contextual and realistic understanding of the practicalities for implementation of school-improvement agendas positions school leaders to design purposeful interactions with the social brain in mind. Emotional intelligence will serve them in leveraging silos through collaborative interactions and seeing diversity as a superpower.

The brain sees *difference* as a threat, which means leading collaboration requires knowledge *and* experience with expertise in content, process, product and environment. Difference regarded as an asset and resource to the organisation is not something that needs to be conformed or removed. However, for leaders to harness the wisdom that is possible in collaborative interactions, intentional investments in relationships are required. Socially intelligent leaders work with knowledge that silos promote like-mindedness, but can become toxic and derail teamwork and collaborative intentions. These leaders also understand that individuals prioritise those closest to them and in this case, other individuals located in the same space because of the limited time available and multiple demands on that time. Wardley Maps are a tool that school leaders can use to problem-solve issues that surround competing tensions for silo mentality and collaboration within school-improvement initiatives. The processes can be used contextually to explore and anticipate needs of different departments, functions and groups.

As a school leader, each chapter throughout this book was designed to lay the foundation to *map your situational context*. Bringing into focus the *number and type of collaborative interactions* that occur throughout a typical week brings attention to the differentiated relationships individuals are trying to maintain. In distributing their energy, effort and attention to whom they determine closest, leads to *disconnections and misconceptions* as a consequence of *competing tensions*. Largely, this is because collaboration is *socially and cognitively* more complex than first thought. An individual's ability to *manage conversations* because it involves understanding another person's mindstate and intentions is *limited to about five* at any one time. However, *cognitive load* is reduced when guesswork is taken out of the *underlying assumptions* at play.

This is particularly pertinent for those individuals who work in multiple teams and the time available is limited to achieve expected outcomes. It is why *collaboration and silos are polarities* that exist in school contexts. Examining the advantages and disadvantages of both allows leaders to *recognise signals* and *disrupt practices* that can become problematic. The issue is that *silos are cocooned within other silos* and, without realising it, leaders can be part of one, too. Exploring and evaluating leadership programs can highlight gaps within their own leader apprenticeship, but consideration of an *insider-outsider* can add value by providing perspectives with a more panoramic view. These neutral eyes can help leaders to identify *silo mentality as constructs of function, knowledge and experience.*

Leading with the Social Brain in Mind is not a panacea, but it puts relationships front and centre of the important work that educators do. Specifically, it implores system and school leaders to explore how social brain theory contributes to the unintended consequences of their own complex organisational contexts.

References

Andrews, JJ, & Rapp, DN (2015). 'Benefits, costs, and challenges of collaboration for learning and memory.' *Translational Issues in Psychological Science, 1*(2), 182–191. https://doi.org/10.1037/tps0000025

Askell-Williams, H, & Koh, G (2020). 'Enhancing the sustainability of school improvement initiatives.' *School Effectiveness and School Improvement, 31*(4), 660–678. https://doi.org/10.1080/09243453.2020.1767657

Australian Institute for Teaching and School Leadership (2014a). *Australian Professional Standard for Principals and the Leadership Profiles.* Education Services Australia. Retrieved from www.aitsl.edu.au/docs/default-source/default-document-library/australian-professional-standard-for-principals-and-the-leadership-profiles652c8891b1e86477b58fff00006709da.pdf?sfvrsn=11c4ec3c_2

Beck, J (2017). 'The Weight of a Heavy Hour: Understanding Teacher Experiences of Work Intensification.' *McGill Journal of Education (Online), 52*(3), 617–636. https://doi.org/10.7202/1050906ar

Bergman, TJ, & Beehner, JC (2015). 'Measuring social complexity.' *Animal Behaviour, 103*, 203–209. https://doi.org/10.1016/j.anbehav.2015.02.018

Biesta, G (2017a). 'Education, Measurement and the Professions: Reclaiming a space for democratic professionality in education.' *Educational Philosophy and Theory, 49*(4), 315–330. https://doi.org/10.1080/00131857.2015.1048665

Boag, RJ, Strickland, L, Loft, S, & Heathcote, A (2019). 'Strategic attention and decision control support prospective memory in a complex dual-task environment.' *Cognition, 191,* 103974–103974. https://doi.org/10.1016/j.cognition.2019.05.011

Cilliers, F, & Greyvenstein, H (2012). 'The impact of silo mentality on team identity: An organisational case study.' *SA Journal of Industrial Psychology, 38*(2), 1–9. https://doi.org/10.4102/sajip.v38i2.993

Cook, N (2008). Enterprise 2.0: 'How Social Software Will Change the Future of Work'

Davenport, T, & Beck, J (2001). *The Attention Economy: Understanding the New Currency of Business.* Harvard Business School Press

Dávid-Barrett, T, & Dunbar, RIM (2013). 'Processing power limits social group size: computational evidence for the cognitive costs of sociality.' *Proc Biol Sci, 280*(1765), 20131151. https://doi.org/10.1098/rspb.2013.1151

Dávid-Barrett, T, & Dunbar, RIM (2016). 'Language as a coordination tool evolves slowly.' *Royal Society Open Science, 3*(12), 160259. https://doi.org/10.1098/rsos.160259

de Jong, K, Moolenaar, N, Osagie, E, & Phielix, C (2016). 'Valuable Connections: A social capital perspective on teachers' social networks, commitment and self-efficacy.' *Pedagogia Social* (28), 71–83. https://doi.org/10.SE7179/PSRL2016.28.06

Dean, K (2010). *Strategies and Benefits of Fostering Intra-Organizational Collaboration.* (Publication Number 15) Marquette University. e-Publications@Marquette

Department of Education and Training (2018b). *Through Growth to Achievement: Report of the Review to Achieve Educational Excellence in Australian Schools.* Canberra Retrieved from https://www.education.gov.au/quality-schools-package/resources/through-growth-achievement-report-review-achieve-educational-excellence-australian-schools

Devereux, L, Melewar, TC, Dinnie, K, & Lange, T (2020). 'Corporate identity orientation and disorientation: A complexity theory perspective.' *Journal of Business Research, 109,* 413–424. https://doi.org/10.1016/j.jbusres.2019.09.048

Donnelly, G (2020). 'Leading Change: The Theory and Practice of Integrative Polarity Work.' *World Futures, 76*(8), 497–518. https://doi.org/10.1080/02604027.2020.1801310

Donohoo, J, & Velasco, M (2016). *The Transformative Power of Collaborative Inquiry: Realizing Change in Schools and Classrooms.* https://doi.org/10.4135/9781071872963

Drago-Severson, E, & Maslin-Ostrowski, P (2018). 'In Translation: School Leaders Learning in and from Leadership Practice While Confronting Pressing Policy Challenges.' *Teachers College Record, 120*(1)

DuFour, R, DuFour, R, Eaker, R, Many, T, & Mattos, M (2017). *Learning by Doing: A Handbook for Professional Learning Communities at Work* (Third ed.). Hawker Brownlow Education

DuFour, R, & Reeves, D (2016). 'The futility of PLC Lite.' *Phi Delta Kappan, 97*(6), 69–71. https://doi.org/10.1177/0031721716636878

Dunbar, RIM (1998). 'The social brain hypothesis.' *Evolutionary Anthropology: Issues, News, and Reviews, 6*(5), 178–190. https://doi.org/10.1002/(SICI)1520-6505(1998)6:5<178::AID-EVAN5>3.0.CO2-8

Dunbar, RIM (2003). 'The Social Brain: Mind, Language, and Society in Evolutionary Perspective.' *Annual Review of Anthropology, 32,* 163–181. https://doi.org/10.1146/annurev.anthro.32.061002.093158

Dunbar, RIM (2010). 'Constraints on the evolution of social institutions and their implications for information flow.' *Journal of Institutional Economics, 7*(03), 345–371. https://doi.org/10.1017/s1744137410000366

Dunbar, RIM (2014a). 'What's So Social About the Social Brain?' In: Decety, J, Christen, Y (eds) *New Frontiers in Social Neuroscience.* Research and Perspectives in Neurosciences, vol 21. Springer, Cham. https://doi-org.ezproxy.usc.edu.au/10.1007/978-3-319-02904-7_1

Dunbar, RIM (2014b). 'The Social Brain: Psychological Underpinnings and Implications for the Structure of Organizations.' *Current Directions in Psychological Science,* 23(2), 109–114. https://doi.org/10.1177/0963721413517118

Dunbar, RIM (2018a). 'The Anatomy of Friendship.' *Trends in Cognitive Sciences,* 22(1), 32–51. https://doi.org/10.1016/j.tics.2017.10.004

Dunbar, RIM, Arnaboldi, V, Conti, M, & Passarella, A (2015). 'The structure of online social networks mirrors those in the offline world.' *Social Networks,* 43, 39–47. https://doi.org/10.1016/j.socnet.2015.04.005

Dunbar, RIM, & Shultz, S (2007). 'Evolution in the Social Brain.' *Science* (American Association for the Advancement of Science), 317(5843), 1344–1347. https://www.science.org/doi/10.1126/science.1145463

Flanagan, T, Grift, G, Lipscombe, K, Wills, J, & Sloper, C (2016). *Transformative Collaboration: 5 Commitments for Leading a Professional Learning Community.* Moorabbin, Vic. Hawker Brownlow Education

Ford, TG, & Youngs, PA (2017). 'Creating organizational structures to facilitate collegial interaction among teachers.' *Educational Management Administration & Leadership,* 46(3), 424–440. https://doi.org/10.1177/1741143216682501

Forsten-Astikainen, R, Hurmelinna-Laukkanen, P, Lämsä, T, Heilmann, P, & Hyrkäs, E (2017). 'Dealing with organizational silos with communities of practice and human resource management.' *Journal of Workplace Learning,* 29(6), 473–489. https://doi.org/10.1108/jwl-04-2015-0028

Fox, A (2010). 'Don't Let Silos Stand in the Way.' *HR Magazine,* 55(5), 50–51

Fullan, M, & Quinn, J (2016). 'Coherence: The Right Drivers in Action for Schools, Districts, and Systems.' *The Teacher,* 54(5), 6

Glen, M, Blackberry, G, & Kearney, J (2017). 'Leading School Improvement, Innovation and Professional Learning Through Action Research: A Policy and Practice Review.' *Leading & Managing,* 23(1), 1–11

Goleman, D (2006). *Social Intelligence: The New Science of Human Relationships.* Hutchinson

Hallinger, P (2018). 'Bringing context out of the shadows of leadership.' *Educational Management, Administration & Leadership,* 46(1), 5–24. https://doi.org/10.1177/1741143216670652

Hargreaves, A, & Fullan, M (2012). *Professional Capital: Transforming Teaching in Every School.* London: Routledge

Hargreaves, A (2019). 'Teacher collaboration: 30 years of research on its nature, forms, limitations and effects.' *Teachers and Teaching, theory and practice,* 25(5), 603–621. https://doi.org/10.1080/13540602.2019.1639499

Haywood-Matty, K (2007). 'From silos to networks: Changing organisations.' *Training and Development in Australia,* 34(5), 15–17

Hogue, M, & Lord, RG (2007). 'A multilevel, complexity theory approach to understanding gender bias in leadership.' *The Leadership quarterly,* 18(4), 370–390. https://doi.org/10.1016/j.leaqua.2007.04.006

Johnson, B (2012). 'The Polarity Approach to Continuity and Transformation.' Polarity Partnerships, LLC

Jones, M, & Harris, A (2014). 'Principals leading successful organisational change.' *Journal of Organizational Change Management, 27*(3), 473–485. https://doi.org/10.1108/jocm-07-2013-0116

Joseph, D, Michael, AK, & Glenn, F (2019). 'Does Size Count Down Under? Australian School Performance, School Size and Public Policy.' *Public administration quarterly, 43*(4), 527–554

Kilgore, SB, & Reynolds, KJ (2011). *From Silos to Systems: Reframing Schools for Success.* Thousand Oaks, Calif.: Corwin Press

Kise, JAG (2014). *Unleashing the Positive Power of Differences: Polarity Thinking in our Schools.* Corwin/Learningforward.

Kolleck, N, Schuster, J, Hartmann, U, & Gräsel, C (2021). 'Teachers' professional collaboration and trust relationships: An inferential social network analysis of teacher teams.' *Research in Education, 111*(1), 89–107. https://doi.org/10.1177/00345237211031585

Leonard, L (2002). 'Schools as Professional Communities: Addressing the Collaborative Challenge.' *International Electronic Journal for Leadership in Learning, 6*(19), n/a

Lewis, PA, Birch, A, Hall, A, & Dunbar, RIM (2017). 'Higher order intentionality tasks are cognitively more demanding.' *Social Cognitive and Affective Neuroscience, 12*(7), 1063–1071. https://doi.org/10.1093/scan/nsx034

Lipton, L, & Wellman, BM (2012). *Got data? Now what? Creating and Leading Cultures of Inquiry.* Solution Tree Press

Lloyd, C (2016). 'Leading Across Boundaries and Silos in a Single Bound.' *Community College Journal of Research and Practice, 40*(7), 607–614. https://doi.org/10.1080/10668926.2015.1125816

Mac Carron, P, Kaski, K, & Dunbar, RIM (2016). 'Calling Dunbar's numbers.' *Social Networks, 47,* 151–155. https://doi.org/10.1016/j.socnet.2016.06.003

Marsh, HW, Dicke, T, Riley, P, Parker, PD, Guo, J, Basarkod, G, & Martin, AJ (2022). 'School principals' mental health and well-being under threat: A longitudinal analysis of workplace demands, resources, burnout, and well-being.' *Applied Psychology: Health and Well-Being.* https://doi.org/10.1111/aphw.12423

Marzano, RJ, Waters, T, & McNulty, BA (2005). *School Leadership that Works: From Research to Results.* Alexandria, Va.: Association for Supervision and Curriculum Development

Musanti, SI, & Pence, L (2010). 'Collaboration and Teacher Development: Unpacking Resistance, Constructing Knowledge, and Navigating Identities.' *Teacher Education Quarterly, 37*(1), 73–89. www.jstor.org.ezproxy.usc.edu.au:2048/stable/23479299

Neebe, AW (1987). 'An Improved, Multiplier Adjustment Procedure for the Segregated Storage Problem.' *Journal of the Operational Research Society, 38*(9), 815–825. https://doi.org/10.1057/jors.1987.135

Pont, B (2020). 'A literature review of school leadership policy reforms.' *European Journal of Education, 55*(2), 154–168. https://doi.org/10.1111/ejed.12398

Saxe, R (2006). 'Uniquely human social cognition.' *Current Opinion in Neurobiology, 16*(2), 235–239. https://doi.org/10.1016/j.conb.2006.03.001

Senge, PM (2012). 'Creating schools for the future, not the past for *all* students.' *Leader to Leader, 2012*(65), 44-49. https://doi.org/10.1002/ltl.20035

Sharratt, L (2018). 'Leading with Knowledge in Communities of Practice.' *Australian Educational Leader, 40*(4), 12-16

Sharratt, L (2019). *Clarity: What Matters Most in Learning, Teaching, and Leading.* Corwin Press

Sharratt, L, & Planche, B (2016). *Leading Collaborative Learning: Empowering Excellence.* Hawker Brownlow Education, Corwin

Sih, A, Hanser, S, & McHugh, K (2009). 'Social network theory: new insights and issues for behavioral ecologists.' *Behavioral Ecology and Sociobiology, 63*(7), 975-988 https://doi.org/10.1007/s00265-009-0725-6

Slater, L (2004). 'Collaboration: A Framework for School Improvement.' *International Electronic Journal for Leadership in Learning, 8,* 1-13

Stone, F (2004). 'Deconstructing silos and supporting collaboration.' *Employment Relations Today, 31*(1), 11-18. https://doi.org/10.1002/ert.20001

Stringfield, S, Reynolds, D, & Schaffer, E (2016). Creating and Sustaining Secondary Schools' Success: Sandfields, Cwmtawe, and the Neath-Port Talbot Local Authority's High Reliability Schools Reform. *Teachers College Record, 118*(13)

Sutcliffe, A, Binder, J, & Dunbar, RIM (2018). 'Activity in social media and intimacy in social relationships.' *Computers in Human Behavior, 85,* 227-235

Sutcliffe, A, Dunbar, RIM, Binder, J, & Arrow, H (2012). 'Relationships and the social brain: Integrating psychological and evolutionary perspectives.' *British Journal of Psychology, 103*(2), 149-168. https://doi.org/10.1111/j.2044-8295.2011.02061.x

Tamarit, I, Cuesta, J, Dunbar, RIM, & Sánchez, A (2018). 'Cognitive resource allocation determines the organization of personal networks.' *Proceedings of the National Academy of Sciences of the United States of America, 115*(33), 8316-8321. https://doi.org/10.1073/pnas.1719233115

Tett, G (2016). *The Silo Effect: Why Every Organisation Needs to Disrupt Itself to Survive.* Abacus

Vangrieken, K, Dochy, F, Raes, E, & Kyndt, E (2015). 'Teacher collaboration: A systematic review.' *Educational Research Review, 15,* 17-40

Vorhaus, J (2014). 'Function and Functional Explanation in Social Capital Theory: A Philosophical Appraisal.' *Studies in Philosophy and Education, 33*(2), 185-199. https://doi.org/10.1007/s11217-013-9380-5

Waal, Ad, Weaver, M, Day, T, & Heijden, Bvd (2019). 'Silo-Busting: Overcoming the Greatest Threat to Organizational Performance.' *Sustainability (Basel, Switzerland), 11*(23), 6860. https://doi.org/10.3390/su11236860

Willcock, DI (2013). *Collaborating for Results: Silo Working and Relationships that Work.* In. Farnham, England; Burlington, Vt. Farnham, Surrey: Farnham, England; Burlington, Vt.: Gower

Wimmer, H, & Perner, J (1983). 'Beliefs about beliefs: Representation and constraining function of wrong beliefs in young children's understanding of deception.' *Cognition, 13*(1), 103-128. https://doi.org/10.1016/0010-0277(83)90004-5